"This book is a huge b
Mina continues to serve, anu ˵˵˵ ˵˵˵˵˵˵ ˵˵˵˵
in this beautiful service, even till now. For a long time, Fr. Mina had the spirit of service living within him; he loved to minister to Christ and consecrate his life to Him. And this matter continues, though he is in heaven. It has expanded, and his abilities are much greater than when he was in the flesh. We are so joyful. Through the prayers of Fr. Mina, and the toils of the author, the Lord has produced a beautiful biography that would gladden the heart of Fr. Mina and allow him to rejoice."

—Mariam Milad Eskander
Wife of Hieromartyr Mina Abood Sharobeem

"The era of martyrdom never ended, as God swore that He would not leave Himself without a witness. The witness of Fr. Mina Abood is a compelling one, precisely because of his 'normalcy.' The blood of the martyrs is still fresh, and Fr. Mina is a hero of faith that deserves to be memorialized. For English readers, what a rare and invaluable gift to have a written record in our mother tongue, delivered so illustriously. I'm grateful to God for this endeavor. It not only takes us through the life of the hieromartyr, but joyfully relives the experience of the author's pilgrimage. The author's ability to help us see through his eyes is uncanny. He helps you smile, struggle, cry and rejoice in real time. May God use this work to the glory of His Name."

—Fr. Antony Paul
Hieromonk, Coptic Orthodox Church;
St. Paul Abbey, Los Angeles, California

"The inspiring story of the life, miracles, and martyrdom of Fr. Mina Abood serves as a beacon of light and hope in a world that has increasingly become filled with darkness and despair. The author, Anthony Marcos, has done a remarkable job outlining the journey of Fr. Mina, from his early life up to his martyrdom. I encourage you to read this book as it will serve as a constant reminder that our Lord does not leave Himself without witness (Acts 14:17)."

—George Bassilios
Professor of apologetics;
author, "Timeless Truth in Truthless Times"

A SPRING IN SINAI

HIEROMARTYR MINA ABOOD

*His **Life**, **Miracles**, and **Martyrdom***
in Post-Revolution Egypt

ANTHONY MARCOS

A Spring in Sinai: Hieromartyr Mina Abood
His Life, Miracles, and Martyrdom in Post-Revolution Egypt

Designed & Published by:
St. Mary & St. Moses Abbey Press
101 S Vista Dr, Sandia, TX 78383
stmabbeypress.com

Funeral photos used by permission of photographers Mina Selim and
Sameh Saad. All other images were provided by courtesy of various sources,
predominantly derived by permission of Sister Mariam, the wife of Hieromartyr
Mina.

Library of Congress Cataloging-in-Publication Data

Names: Marcos, Anthony, 1997- author.
Title: A spring in Sinai: Hieromartyr Mina Abood : his life, miracles, and
     martyrdom in post-revolution Egypt / by Anthony Marcos.
Description: Sandia, TX : St. Mary & St. Moses Abbey Press,
     [2021] | Includes bibliographical references.
Identifiers: LCCN 2020052013 (print) | LCCN 2020052014 (ebook) |
     ISBN 9781939972316 (paperback) | ISBN 9781939972323 (ebook)
Subjects: LCSH: Sharobeem, Mina Abood. |
     Sharobeem, Mina Abood—Miracles. |
     Coptic Church—Clergy—Biography. | Christian martyrs—Egypt—Biography.
Classification: LCC BX139.S57 M37 2021 (print) | LCC BX139.S57 (ebook) |
     DDC 272/.9092 [B]—dc23
LC record available at https://lccn.loc.gov/2020052013
LC ebook record available at https://lccn.loc.gov/2020052014

For Sister Mariam, Verina, and Youstina

Contents

Foreword   xi

Introduction   1

ONE   Early Life to Marriage   12

TWO   Priesthood and Ministry   39

THREE   Revolution, Revelation, and Martyrdom   63

FOUR   Visions and Apparitions   123

FIVE   Anecdotes, Miracles, and
Commemoration   141

Bibliography   177

Acknowledgements

I render thanks to the Lord for His abundant mercies and wonders, which were wholly evident to me in the process of writing this biography. I pray that He be glorified through this book and constantly establish within our hearts the desire to "do all for the glory of God" (1 Cor 10:31).

All gratefulness is due to my cherished mother and friend, Sister Mariam Milad. Words fail me when I attempt to offer you gratitude for your never-ending aid in the production of this work. Thank you for your hospitality during our many hours together, and for trusting me enough to author your martyred husband's biography for the very first time. You are the means by which the world will become acquainted with Fr. Mina. This book is meant to extend the rays of light of his life into the darkened horizons of the diaspora, and illuminate my own dimmed soul.

My most sincere gratitude goes to my beloved spiritual fathers, His Grace Bishop Youssef and His Grace Bishop Eklemandos; without Your Graces, this book would not have come to fruition in the first place. My dear Fr. Jerome, I thank Your Reverence for the incessant prayers and guidance. To each member of my loving family, thank you for your patience and support throughout the time I spent compiling this account. George, James, and John, your toils and encouragement have not gone unnoticed, and I am sure this book would have been greatly lacking without your aid.

The Lord God will certainly recompense you for your efforts, through Hieromartyr Mina's supplications on your behalf.

Foreword

And though in the sight of men, they suffered
torments, their hope is full of immortality. Like
gold in the furnace, He has proved them, and as
a holocaust victim, He has received them, and in
the time of their visitation they will shine, and
they will dash about like sparks among stubble.
(Wis 3:4, 6–7)

I quoted the above passage from the book of Wisdom as
a good illustrative summary of the life of all Christian
martyrs, including Fr. Mina Abood, whose life is the subject
of this blessed book.

In fact, the martyrdom of any Christian martyr is not a
mere incidence that takes place in the last few minutes of his
life. It is rather an "all day long" response to a call to be killed
for the sake of Jesus Christ (Rom 8:36). Therefore, all true
Christians are martyrs even if they are not literally killed.
Every faithful Christian is a cross-bearer in every moment of
his life. This is clearly shown in the life of Fr. Mina Abood as
illustrated in this blessed book. Though Fr. Mina served in
the capacity of holy priesthood for a very short period, yet
this does not mean he stopped serving after being killed. In

fact, his martyrdom introduced him to serving in a much greater capacity in heaven.

As a priest regularly celebrating the Liturgy, he used to offer the sacrifice of his Master on the altar. Eventually, he ended up offering himself as a precious sacrifice acceptable by his Redeemer!

He was offering up incense upon the altar mixed with his fervent prayers for his congregation, and yet, by accepting martyrdom, he himself became a sweet aroma whose smell pleased the Father's heart!

He was interceding for his congregation before the altar by words and groanings, but now, the voice of his blood cries out to the Father interceding not only for the Church, but also for the entire world!

Fr. Mina was fond of hymns; martyrdom turned his own life to become a sweet inspiring hymn that will be chanted by upcoming generations. It also allowed him to join the heavenly angelic choirs in their continuous praises!

He was loyal to his beloved intercessor and friend, St. Stephen the archdeacon and protomartyr and established a hymnological school after his name. St. Stephen, in his turn, honored him by receiving him among the ranks of his successive martyrs!

Truly, the Holy Spirit created every martyr as a unique masterpiece that reflects a real image of God's love and providence.

I am really fascinated by the great dedication and precision of the author of this book, our blessed son Anthony Marcos, who accurately compiled valuable first-hand accounts about the life of Fr. Mina during a trip to

Egypt in the summer of 2019. This account has, by God's grace, become the first biography of Fr. Mina Abood written in English, and the most extensive and thoroughly produced one in any language. I pray to the Lord to bless him and give him the heavenly reward according to what is written, "He who receives a righteous man in the name of a righteous man shall receive a righteous man's reward" (Mt 10:41).

I also pray to the Lord to blaze the fire of His love in the hearts of this book's readers, to fortify their faith, and to accept the prayers of Fr. Mina among the prayers of all the martyrs for us all. To whom is glory forever and ever. Amen.

Bishop Youssef
Bishop of the Coptic Orthodox Diocese
of the Southern United States

Introduction

Slogging through the wilderness, the Israelites were on the cusp of death, trudging through the sand in the inhospitable deserts of Sinai. As far as they were concerned, their breaths in the desert were soon to become their last, as their "prophet" seemed to be recklessly guiding them to their doom, just outside the glimmering Egyptian borders. There was no water for the people to drink.

"Give us water that we may drink.... Why is it you have brought us up out of Egypt, to kill us and our children ... with thirst?"

"Why do you contend with me? Why do you tempt the Lord?" He would ask, confounded by their questioning whether the benevolent Lord was truly among them or not.

As the Israelite refugees felt the scorching heat bake them like clay, they continued to plead and hurl insults at their stammering prophet, and they almost looked ready to hurl stones at him too.

He lifted his gaze to heaven and sought refuge in God, and His counsel. Then the prophet took a few elders of the people with him, and approached the rock of Horeb. He lunged his arm forward, and struck his rod into its heart. Surely to the amazement and bewilderment of those present, a fountain of water began to gush from an otherwise normal-looking rock, and the people were given a means of quenching their thirst from the pool of water forming in the desert.

I remember it being an oppressively hot day in the summer of 2013 when the disturbing news reached me in the United States. The Egypt-wide chaos aroused the cold-blooded murder of a priest in that very same Sinai.

Thousands of miles away from me, a swarm of local villagers gathered around the convulsing body of this clergyman, whose blood began to pool around his head. There, in the wilderness of Sinai, the people of God gathered around as they yearned to satisfy their thirst for justice, equality, human rights, and living without fear of continual persecution and discrimination. And there, in Sinai, a rock was yet again struck, out of which sprung a fountain in the arid desert, irrigated by the blood of this holy father.

Strewn across Arabic news channels, newspapers, and media outlets I saw a photograph of the presbyter. He seemed young, maybe in his thirties, I assumed. His beard was scarcely beyond a five o'clock shadow; the man had barely gotten a sufficient chance to serve the altar, I thought. He stood at a pulpit with his kind eyes raised on high, and his mouth was partially open, evidently chanting.

Though I fully and completely recognized his status as a hieromartyr,[1] I recall thinking within myself, "He honestly seems like a normal guy."

Fr. Mina Abood Sharobeem indeed was just a normal, relatable young man.

The complaints of the people who could not see their God in the desert were now answered by this "normal guy" who, lying lifelessly in the street, proclaimed with each of his bullet wounds the astounding message of peace and life found in the midst of chaos—the message of love, sacrifice, and a martyr's death.

I had only been a college graduate for a few months when I went away for a retreat to visit my spiritual father, His Grace Bishop Eklemandos, during an annual trip to Cairo, a trip he would meticulously draw up an itinerary for every time I set foot in the bustling city. On a quiet evening at the bishop's residence, over two cups of tea, His Grace and I sat at the dinner table, where he explained to me that before his ordination to the bishopric, he was delegated to serve as a hieromonk in Sinai.

"That reminds me," he excitedly whispered, grabbing my arm, "why don't we have you visit Tasoni[2] Mariam, the wife of Fr. Mina Abood?"

I smiled and replied, "Why not?"

---

1   A hieromartyr is a martyr who was also a member of the clergy. The prefix of this title (hiero) is originally from the Greek adjective *hierós* (ἱερός), which means sacred or sanctified, consecrated to God and set apart for service to Him. The derivative noun of this word—*hiereús* (ἱερεύς)—is used in the New Testament to refer to priests (e.g., Mt 12:4; Mk 1:44; Lk 1:5; Jn 1:19; Acts 4:1; 6:7; Heb 7 [several verses]).

2   Tasoni is the transliteration of the Coptic word meaning "sister," which is the common title used to address the wife of a priest in the Coptic Orthodox Church.

He quickly jotted down the "holy site," adding it to the list he had composed as part of the itinerary he situated for me, and had his secretary Kerlous call Tasoni to set up an appointment.

With the phone call on speaker, I overheard her kindly and excitedly respond to the secretary's request: "Of course! Fr. Mina's home is Anthony's home!"

The following morning, I got dressed and waited for His Grace; he would surely accompany me to visit Sister Mariam, as he did on every pilgrimage of mine. Emerging from his cell, His Grace strangely apologized, "I won't come with you today; I'll send Kerlous with you."

As a youth, Kerlous also lived in Sinai, and took Fr. Mina as a spiritual father during the year and four months in which he served as a priest. I was told he was even with the hieromartyr on the night of his death. Kerlous was enthusiastic to accompany me, and I was relieved that a mutual friend of Fr. Mina and his wife would come along.

The trip to her apartment was agitating. The arid Egyptian heat swallowed me whole in the long, suffocating car ride through the dense and chaotic city, where my own thoughts were drowned out by the incessant honking.

Why hadn't the bishop come with me?

Coming out of the elevator, I was immediately greeted with a life-size portrait of Fr. Mina plastered on the wall next to the apartment's front door. He glimmered with a friendly smile, as if he was welcoming me to his home; in fact, it was relieving. At the sound of my timid knocks on her door, Sister Mariam opened for us and received us in.

Sister Mariam's demeanor was my first impression of Fr.

Mina. I was taken aback to find her dressed in all white. In front of me was an Egyptian widow (who typically would drape herself in somber black) living in an apartment filled to the brim with reminders of her slaughtered love. But she beamed with an unusually ascetic joy. She might as well have been a nun (she even sported a veil over her head, constantly covering her hair in the similitude of a monastic). Attempting to grasp her countenance held my tongue to my throat for a second.

She proudly wore a small portrait of her husband around her neck; it hung with such glory, as though she were presenting to me a victor of war. The first time I saw that very picture, I was sitting comfortably almost 7,000 miles away in the United States, dissociated from the reality of his bloodshed. But now, I felt closer to him than I could have ever imagined. This victor's photo hung next to a bold and beautiful cross—the emblem of the Conqueror, the Head of conquerors.

Walking in, I was instantly riveted by the reliquary in her living room: a sizable glass display case enclosed some very sacred vestments of this martyred priest, who had now become my host for the day. A table nearby carried some other small reliquaries, one with the relics of my wonder-working host, and another, which, I was told, was literally God-sent.

On that same table also lay some of Fr. Mina's belongings; I picked up a small knitted cap which belonged to him. Sister Mariam recounted how several miraculous healings were done by the Lord for those who wore the cap I was holding in my hands. I soon came to realize, this home was a piece of heaven, and there was more to Fr. Mina than meets the eye.

"I'm always the happiest when I talk about my love," she smiled. "However, I want you to know that Fr. Mina was just a normal guy."

I was sincerely confused.

I saw reliquaries that smelled of fragrant spices, which are traditionally prepared over the relics of saintly people whose (sometimes admittedly overly romanticized) stories I grew up hearing. I saw images of this priest hung up on every wall, many of them having a halo edited into the photo.

Sister Mariam's words were juxtaposed with what my eyes were seeing, and I grew puzzled. "I'll explain everything," she assured me while bursting into an innocent belly laugh, before beginning to reverently explain the hagiography of her beloved husband.

His story was as transparent and as candid as can possibly be. It was unlike any of the ones I had ever heard. Sister Mariam narrated Fr. Mina's human struggles, as well as his saintly virtues. She disclosed his doubts, which, at one point, pressured him to abandon an increasingly durable ministry, as well as his triumphs over these doubts. She described how she knew him to be occasionally faint-hearted, and yet she also recounted his remarkable bravery as a fully automatic gun was aimed to the side of his head.

It was almost biblical. Consider the illustrious Moses for example—he was not "perfect." A moment of anger turned him into a murderer and a wanted vagabond. The tablets of the law, carved into cold slabs of stone with the very fingers of God, were smashed in another moment of unrestrained wrath. A debilitating stutter had mercilessly grabbed him by the lips and brought his self-esteem to the dust. Even Moses himself doubted the sensibility of God's calling due to his many perceived weaknesses.

As Sister Mariam narrated her husband's virtues, Moses's sister Miriam singing the praises of her brother's victory came to mind. The stampede of vicious charioteers and the great bows and arrows of the golden Pharaoh drowned—drowned in the Red Sea.

The threatening demands of the murderers of Fr. Mina also drowned in a red sea that the saintly priest poured out in front of his parish church. He stood in the face of armed militants, and with the breath of God's grace, conquered the impending doom of death itself.

Sainthood is reached when the Lord, by the breath of His grace, perfects our own imperfections. And often the seemingly simplest of gestures yield profound outcomes. Moses raised his arms and his staff, prophesying the open arms Christ would show the world on Golgotha in His display of victory. And Fr. Mina took that victory and embraced it—all with a simple, "No."

Though the world may pressure us with gold or silver, precious offers to adopt this religion or that, to bow to this idol and embrace that one, Fr. Mina only said, "No." And the strength to do so did not come from a vow of monasticism, nor did he have to storm the palace of the magistrate and curse a few stone idols to show an open refusal to apostatize. He simply stood near his humble abode, the little local church in the streets of Sinai, and was killed in cold blood in broad daylight, because the truth does not hide in the darkness of night.

So this mysterious hieromartyr had me wondering.

What if the man across from me at the coffee shop is being forged into a saint? Or the one who cut me off in traffic? Fr. Mina proved to me that sainthood is attainable, and that the Lord is able to work with our many imperfections—if we let Him.

I returned back to the bishop's residence very late that evening and we sipped some tea again.

I boldly asked, "Why didn't Your Grace come with us today? Were you busy?"

The room fell silent.

He replied bluntly, "No. Frankly, I'm somewhat angry with Fr. Mina."

"... angry?"

Covering the obvious crack in his voice with another sip from his mug, he reminded me, "I used to serve in the area in which Fr. Mina served."

He paused, drawing in a breath.

"His crown was supposed to be mine!"

Here was a bishop before me, complaining of being so close to donning an unfading crown of martyrdom. And it was with that when I realized, we are all "so close."

The Christian is called to run through the streets of this world after the kingdom of God, but the kingdom of God ran to Fr. Mina in the streets of Sinai. This warrior was given the spoils of combat by every bullet he willingly absorbed. Every drop of blood which fell from him screamed testimonies of his faith to his bewildered onlookers.

Tertullian, the prolific apologist of the early Church, portrays the blood of the martyrs as being like a seed of the

Church, inspiring its growth rather than its demise;[3] and now I write to you from a garden—the lush, paradisiacal Church. The red and bloody fruit of the Vine, which once ran down the wood of the cross, now runs down our stiff and wooden hearts, making them flow with life once more. When, in weakness, our minds overlook this, the ever-spilling blood of the Christian martyrs serves to remind us of Christ's inconceivable sacrifice, which was offered to vivify His creation. His blood, shed for the sake of love, gave us life; their blood, shed for the sake of Love Himself, encourages us to live out lives of heartening renewal.

St. Theophan the Recluse[4] speaks of how a Christian who "refuses to give into his passions does the same as he who refuses to bow down and worship idols."[5] He goes on to explain:

> He who refused to worship idols was given over to external sufferings, while he who refuses to satisfy the passions actually wounds himself and forces his heart to suffer until the passions quiet down in him. Victory over passions is a self-inflicted spiritual martyrdom, which is performed invisibly in the heart but is nevertheless very painful. When you gave your vows to serve the Lord, what did you promise? You promised to: Divest yourselves of the old man, which is decomposing in sinful passions ... and be

---

3   cf. Tertullian *The Apology* 50.13.

4   Bishop of Tambov, Russia, who departed January 6, 1894, and was canonized by the Russian Orthodox Church in 1988.

5   A homily delivered by St. Theophan the Recluse to the nuns of the Ascension Convent in the city of Tambov, Russia. In *Kindling the Divine Spark* (Platina, CA: Saint Herman Press, 1994), 39.

vested in the new man, created according to God's righteousness and true holiness (Ephesians 4:22, 24). The old man is completely composed of passions. The divesting of it means spiritual martyrdom.

If this is the case, is a bold confession of the faith really that far off? In turn, is martyrdom itself so unachievable? If not chosen for literal bloodshed, a Christian is called to be metaphorically slaughtered, engaging in an on-going war with the world. Only then does he merit wearing the crown encrusted with the precious stones of his struggles. Several fathers have shared similar sentiments regarding the notion of "bloodless martyrdom." St. John Chrysostom, for example, urged Christians:

> Mortify your body, and crucify it, and you will yourself receive the crown of martyrdom. For what in the other case the sword accomplishes [against one's will], then in this case, let a willing mind [accomplish the same].[6]

Likewise, St. Augustine taught "Let no one say 'I cannot be a martyr because there is now no persecution.'"[7]

If we walk in the light, as children of the light, the assaults of darkness are unavoidable and inevitable. Vanity targets us with every single step toward an eternity of repose. We

6 John Chrysostom Homilies on Hebrew 11.6. In Paul Middleton, *Martyrdom: A Guide for the Perplexed* (London, ENG: T&T Clark International, 2011), 84–85.

7 Augustine *Sermon on Martyrdom*. Ibid.

are enlisted in a war that is both unseen and unequaled. Let us not lose heart. In riding into the war with a triumphant spirit, following the example of our Commander (who is appropriately described as a "Man of war" by Moses himself),[8] and placing before us the examples of the honest soldiers who preceded us to the kingdom, we can become victors too.

You who search for the company of the saints and question their presence in the world today, this work is dedicated to you.

You who wish to be acquainted with the youthful priest who is arguably among the greatest contemporary martyrs to be birthed by the Coptic Orthodox Church of Alexandria, this work is dedicated to you.

You who call the diaspora home, and are besieged by lukewarmness in spirituality, deficient in holy encouragement, this work is dedicated to you.

I earnestly pray that what you will be exposed to within the pages of this "normal" account may compel you to progress toward the abnormal levels of sanctity you are called to assume.

May this wonder-working father prayerfully remember you by name.

Fight.

And water the desert of Sinai that engulfs you.

---

8   Exodus 15:3

CHAPTER ONE

Early Life to Marriage

Birth and Upbringing

On Saturday, December 14, 1974, at an hour past midnight, a young boy was born to an Upper Egyptian family hailing from the depths of the lands of Aswan.

Several months prior to his birth, his mother, Fayka Ghattas Andrawis, had a puzzling dream, in which a man appeared and stood before her silently. Within moments, he extended his right arm upwards and revealed his tattoo of a cross on his wrist, a common tradition among Egypt's Copts.

However, this man's cross differed from the standard traditional tattoo in that it was uniquely large, extending down the length of his forearm. The man disappeared, and Fayka arose from her sleep, informing her family that she would name her child "Saleeb," meaning "cross" in the Arabic language, after the beautiful cross on her mysterious visitor's arm.

She was met with absolute disagreement from her family, even her father confessor, a certain Fr. Boutros, who insisted that the child would suffer in the Islamic society he was to grow up in. Fayka was recommended to consider opting for the Greek equivalent *stavros* instead, so as to avoid the otherwise conspicuous association of this boy's name and his religion.

In courage, standing up against her kin, she announced that if the goal was to avoid the declaration of the Christian faith, then she would not heed their suggestions. The boy, who would eventually carry the cross of torture and martyrdom, suffering in similitude of his Master, was named after that very cross—Saleeb Abood Sharobeem.

Crawling in the dust of Upper Egypt, soaking in her distinctive sunshine, and drinking the water of her Nile, Saleeb grew in a typical Coptic Orthodox Christian family. He was raised by two God-fearing parents who reared him in the Orthodox faith. His father, Abood Sharobeem, worked as an engineer; he never ceased in extending his abilities for the service of the Church.

His mother, Fayka, raised three children—among whom Saleeb was the eldest—in the utmost fear of God, instilling in them the love of Orthodoxy, especially the sacraments with which the Church is adorned. Saleeb grew to love the Church and found it a beloved pastime, spending long hours of the day within its walls, reading in the Sanctuary, and being saturated by his mere presence in the house of God. He stood out by his possessing a calm, meek demeanor as compared to his two younger brothers, Mina and John. His mother could hardly recall a single time in which she found Saleeb badly behaving, atypical of course for children

13

at that age.

In the third year of Saleeb's preparatory education, his father departed to Paradise as a result of a horrific car accident, which also killed two others in the vehicle with him. Fayka was left alone to raise her three children as a young widow. She did so successfully, continuing to rear them in the love of the Holy Trinity. Losing their father was indeed distressing for the growing boys, especially their eldest; Saleeb was found to have been affected greatest by his father's sudden death. In the loss of his only father-figure, Saleeb found another father—the "Father of orphans and protector of widows" (Ps 68:5).

Saleeb drew closer to the bosom of the Church and found his comfort and solace in the midst of sorrow by attending the Divine Liturgy as much as he was capable. It was this event that fashioned a love for the holy altar within the heart of the young child, later making way for the child to serve the altar in a life of consecration, completely encased by clouds of incense and reverberations of liturgical hymns.

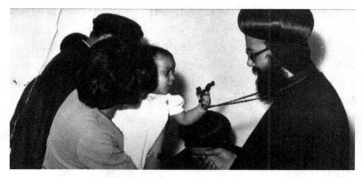

The child Saleeb Abood with His Eminence Metropolitan Hedra

Saleeb in the company of his parents, Abood and Fayka,
and his younger brothers, Mina and John, before the
relics of St. Abraam, Bishop of Al Faiyum, Egypt

Youth

Akin to what was said of our Savior, Saleeb "grew in wisdom
and stature, and in favor with God and man" (Lk 2:52).
He moved on to his secondary education, and this marked
the start of his involvement in the service at his local parish
named after the Theotokos St. Mary, in Aswan, Egypt.

It was obvious that an interest in the ancient hymns of
the Coptic Orthodox Church had grasped Saleeb by the
hand, and it led him under the feet of his church's cantor,
Raghib Abdou. He became familiarized with the hymns,

some of which find their roots in millennia of rich Orthodox history.

Saleeb was described as seeking and chanting hymns not out of habit as many of us feel, but rather out of true, legitimate love for God. He would be seen actually running through the streets in excitement with his friends, all enthusiastically making their way to church to attend their weekly hymns class. Saleeb unfailingly attended the Midnight Praises on Saturday evening on a weekly basis, irrespective of his circumstances, whether related to his education or to his need to care for the household. If he was found to be ill, he would leave his bed and attend the praises; if an exam was to be written the next morning, he would close his books and spend the evening praising in his church. There was hardly an impediment that could get in his way.

"I will sing praise to Your name forever, that I
may daily perform my vows" (Ps 61:8)

Such a dedication never failed him, and the Lord led him to success due to his relentless attitude of allotting time to grow spiritually. In his mind, this is what mattered, and all else was secondary.

His mother described a humorous account that demonstrated how Saleeb designated his priorities: Exam season in his last year before the start of university approached, and while his peers hit the books, Saleeb instead sat in his room for hours listening to recordings of hymns chanted by the renowned Coptic cantors Mikhail Al Batanouny[9] and Ibrahim Ayad,[10] which he stored in a collection of hundreds of cassettes he had gathered over the years. His mother ordered him to leave the cassettes and open his books and pick up on hymns again once his

---

9   Mikhail Girgis Al Batanouny (1873–1957), commonly referred to as, "Mikhail the Great," was the leader of cantors of the Great Cathedral in Cairo, an expert in Coptic rites and music, and is pivotal in the preservation of Coptic hymnology, being the first to record them via audio recordings in their original form.

10 Ibrahim Ayad is presently the lead cantor of the Great Cathedral in Cairo, serving as one of the Coptic Orthodox Church's main authoritative figures in Coptic hymnology.

vacation began. She would tell him, "Render to Caesar the things that are Caesar's, and to God the things that are God's" (Mk 12:17). Later that night, she walked into his room and found him hiding under his bed covers with a Walkman cassette player to his ear, covertly listening to yet another cassette of hymns!

The next morning, his mother sought out His Eminence Metropolitan Hedra, Metropolitan of the Diocese of Aswan, who had grown significantly closer to the family after the death of Abood. She complained to the Metropolitan about how his spiritual son, Saleeb, disregarded his studies and focused on hymns. Metropolitan Hedra, in response, laughed, "Madame Fayka, are we now complaining about both those who are close to and far from God? Leave him to do as he pleases!" Many contemporary issues plague families, especially in such a formative age of their children's lives, which often lead them to complain to clergy. But as for this blessed child, in his purity and virtue, he sought to become acquainted with the language of the heavenly.

Saleeb did not stop at merely attending the Midnight Praises or learning its hymns. He began encouraging his peers at St. Mary's church in Aswan to join in the hymns also. He quickly assembled a group of youth to gather and pray the Midnight Praises on Tuesday and Saturday on a weekly basis. Furthermore, in order to include everyone, Saleeb obtained the approval of Metropolitan Hedra to hold the Midnight Praises at an earlier hour than usual on Thursday evenings in order to involve all the young women who wanted to attend and learn but could not stay out late due to their household curfews.

Move to Cairo

At the age of twenty, Saleeb hosted his uncle, Kamal Ghattas, who suggested that he move from Aswan to Cairo and continue his university education there, though he had already been accepted to the University of Sohag in Upper Egypt. Indeed, his uncle submitted an application on his behalf to the University of Ain Shams, Faculty of Trade and Commerce, as Saleeb's legal guardian. So, having been accepted, in 1994 Saleeb moved to Cairo and lived with his uncle.

He was described as having rarely studied during the period of time in his uncle's house. Rather, as was his habit, he was keen on listening to his collection of cassettes of hymns and homilies by Pope Shenouda III which he brought with him from Aswan. He would sit his cousins down and teach them the hymns he had learned, until they, too, were introduced to the depth of Orthodox hymnology and the love of the Church that accompanied it.

The first task Saleeb carried out upon his arrival to Cairo was to locate the nearest parish to his uncle's residence—the church of the Theotokos St. Mary in Al Amiriya. The parish priest, Fr. Girgis Nathan, describes his first encounter with Saleeb:

> One day I was sitting in my office, and a meek young man knocked and walked in, introducing himself as Saleeb Abood, a student coming from Aswan to study in the University of Ain Shams. He was in need of a new father confessor due to his move from his hometown. From the very first meeting, I had become

familiar with the fact that the youth before me was godly to a rare extent.

He procured a God-given ability to memorize, using it to learn the rarest of Church hymns, even those unknown by the vast majority of deacons. I also later noticed his unique voice which led the entire congregation into a prayerful atmosphere during every service. He related to me his passionate love for the Midnight Praises, as well as the services he undertook in handing down the hymns to the younger generations back in his home parish.

I will reveal that I had been praying to the Lord to send me a servant to revive the service of the hymns and the Midnight Praises in my parish for a while; I do admit that it had grown somewhat weak and had diminished. When this youth walked into my office, I indeed felt that he was not a mere student, but an answer to a heartfelt prayer.

Saleeb Abood Sharobeem

Indeed it was described that the service of teaching hymnology, as well as the service of the differing ranks of the diaconate in the church of St. Mary in Al Amiriya lacked, to the point that several generations were deprived of proper hymnological education; many were accustomed to either stand in the church absent-minded as to what was being chanted, or avoid the services involving praises altogether.

By the grace of God, Saleeb wasted no time in attending the Divine Liturgies, becoming involved in his new parish. In this manner, he befriended the youth and organized a method by which to hand down the hymns he received at the hands of the cantors who taught him previously.

As if he was a gift sent from heaven, Saleeb revived this service in the parish; he started with a small number of both young men and women, only about five individuals. However, as the five loaves in the hands of the Lord, they grew and thrived, feeding the multitudes. As a seed in a fertile ground tilled by the Great Sower, they grew into a tree with branches which provided shade to several generations who were able to more fully savor the sweetness of Orthodoxy.

Taking the Lord as his guide, Saleeb founded the Chorus of David the Prophet, which comprised of twenty-five servants, each handing down the hymns to dozens of children.

Sister Mariam Milad describes the very first time she saw her would-be husband, Saleeb, and the start of his ministry in her home parish:

We would hold Midnight Praises every Tuesday and Saturday at the church of St. Mary [in Al Amiriya]. We never had anyone teach us the hymns of the Midnight Praises, so a very small minority would be chanted in the Coptic language—maybe some of the canticles, and the rest of the service would be chanted fully in Arabic—we didn't know it!

One day, on a Saturday evening, we found a meek-looking youth standing among us, and in a unique, beautiful voice, this youth fully versed the praises with us in Coptic, and in its full tune!

We noticed he didn't look at a book the entire time. It reminded us of the monks in the monasteries, who knew the Midnight Praises like the backs of their hands.

Of course, seeing a youth like this amazed us, and we all surrounded him and insisted he teach us everything he knows; he did not hesitate to agree. He held an informal class for us, and in all honesty, we could sit with him for four hours and not grow weary. We would take breaks in the middle only because our voices would get tired. Due to his love for hymnology, he delivered the hymn he was teaching in a beautiful spirit, and in a manner that was not dull.

Saleeb would teach and say, "Learn the hymns, for they are the language of heaven; learn them, so you may one day be capable of living with the angels, of living in continuous praises."

As a first-year university student, Saleeb successfully founded the Chorus of David the Prophet, and yet his soul hungered for more. He yearned to convey the love of hymnology to a greater number. In 2006, he suggested an idea to his parish priest, Fr. Girgis: starting a school fully dedicated to teaching hymns. He was noted as being an individual, who, upon discovering an idea that would aid the service, was determined to carry the idea out, regardless of any outside factors; he did not let impeding considerations—such as monetary constraints, or logistics regarding where the school would be located—dishearten or worry him. He left all such concerns in the hands of God, the benevolent Lord who can be trusted to support the endeavor so long as the objective is the service of His holy name. By God's grace, Saleeb secured a heartfelt approval from Fr. Girgis and began his work in founding the St. Stephen the Archdeacon Hymns School.

The school included students of all ages, from children

in preschool up to university and graduate students. It began with 20 male and female teachers (those discipled under Saleeb) and eventually expanded to over sixty teachers.

The school continued to grow at an incredibly fast pace, prompting the church to purchase a property located directly behind it in order to accommodate the increasing need. Currently, the St. Stephen the Archdeacon Hymns School hosts approximately five-hundred students. It began with offering limited courses in hymnology and the Coptic language, but now offers a variety of courses encompassing also liturgical rites, Church history, and dogmatic studies.

Among the astonishing situations that occurred in relation to the school was that one day a weeping mother entered the school, lamenting through her tears that her four-year-old daughter had not returned home after her afternoon class. Upon being told by the mother that she would hold him responsible for the lost child, Saleeb, in the company of many servants, took to the streets of Al Amiriya in search of the girl.

Desperate for help, Saleeb broke down in the middle of the street. Looking up to heaven with tears in his eyes, he prayed, "St. Stephen, the school is named after you. Please return the girl!" Within moments, he had received a call that the child had safely arrived home.

Saleeb and the servants with him immediately made their way to the little girl's home and asked her how she found her way. She related in all simplicity, "I was in the street, and a man dressed in a deacon's tunic, with two red stripes on his shoulders, took me by the hand and led me to my house." It was realized that the child's guide was the intercessor of the school, St. Stephen himself. The servants rejoiced greatly and, upon completing the visit, returned to the church where many candles were lit before the icon of the saint and many praises were offered, thanking the Lord for His care for His children.

In Saleeb's mind, the service was a means for God's glorification. In that sense, he never worried, especially when it came to matters regarding the school's budget and expenses. A servant in the school, who was given the responsibility of collecting donations and managing the school's budgeting, explains that on the occasions that she was tasked with purchasing the gifts for the school children, especially around the time of the Feast of the Nativity, she would barely find any money. Whenever she would express her concerns to Saleeb, he would tell her to buy the gifts, assuring her that the Lord would be responsible for the costs. Barely any time would pass before she would receive a message from Saleeb telling her to go to the church, where she would find a man waiting for her to give her a donation. On every occasion this occurred, the donation she received would cover exactly what was needed to purchase the gifts.

Another service that Saleeb was keen on involved encouraging the youth he served to visit the many monasteries of the Egyptian desert for spiritual retreat, particularly those in the renowned region of Scetis. He would even offer to drive them to the monasteries and be their companion in the retreat.

It happened once that Saleeb had approached a youth to join him on a pilgrimage to the Monastery of St. Macarius the Great. The youth refused, saying, "Your car is known to overheat quickly, and I don't want to be stuck sleeping in the desert tonight!" Saleeb simply responded that the Lord would take care of them.

The youth was convinced, and together, they headed to the Monastery of St. Macarius. Their time there was deeply edifying. Saleeb was described as seeming like he did not want to part from the monastery and return to the world. On their way back to Cairo, Saleeb's car did indeed overheat, to the point that it stalled in the middle of the desert road and began emitting smoke from under the hood.

The youth yelled, "Saleeb! The car's on fire!"

"Have no fear," Saleeb replied calmly, "St. Macarius won't allow for anything bad to befall us."

The youth was told to stay in the car, while Saleeb was to take a look under the hood. The youth could not see what Saleeb was doing due to the hood obscuring the view from inside. After an extended period of time had passed, he exited the car to check on Saleeb, only to find him kneeling on the sand before the car. Approaching him, the youth heard him whispering the psalms. Saleeb rose to his feet and produced a picture of St. Macarius from his pocket. He placed the picture on the engine of the car. Closing the hood on top of the picture, he chuckled, "We'll let St. Macarius take care of this." They both entered the car once more, and Saleeb was miraculously able to start the car again and drive it to the nearest gas station (which was about a thirty-minute drive away) where a mechanic was able to repair the problem.

His Work and Relationship with His Colleagues

In 1997, Saleeb graduated from the University of Ain Shams and completed his degree in Trade and Commerce, taking an accounting position in one of Cairo's companies. When searching for a job, his priority was to find a position that gave him freedom to spend his leisure time in the service of the church. He lived in simplicity, not seeking or caring for salaries and promotions, but rather turning his attention to how he would spend his time so that his soul may be quenched by the many fountains that flowed from the house of God.

Saleeb's adherence to God in turn yielded rivers of living water that were evident in several of his virtues. He was loyal in his work and possessed a work-ethic that demonstrated the faithfulness our Savior asks of us. He maintained an amazing relationship with each of his colleagues, Christian and non-Christian alike. He was incredibly cheerful, to the point that his coworkers explained that his smile was enough to make their whole day. Above all, he was described as never starting or partaking in a conversation that included speaking ill of a coworker; he was keen on never falling into gossip. Every coworker Saleeb dealt with felt that he became a personal friend to them. This allowed them to feel comfortable enough to open up to him and seek his advice regarding their personal issues.

He was loved by all and loved all. He practiced pastoral care even before being ordained for such a responsibility. For example, on several occasions he would walk into work and see one of his colleagues absent; he would then make it a point to call them to be reassured that they were okay.

While it may be common for people to express the need to "pass the time" at work, Saleeb strove to invest each minute to "redeem the time" (Eph 5:16) and not waste a moment. And if a moment of free time came, he would use it open his Bible which he kept in his desk, or bring up the Bible on the computer, in order to become sated by His living word.

He carried his Lord within him, allowing Him to shine wherever he worked. He displayed the image of the genuine Christian amidst a world tainted by falseness and corrupted by cheating and deceit. How beautiful it is to carry our Holy Christ into every place we enter! The world around us is in great want of a noble, living example who rarely uses words but instead acts according to faithfulness, truthfulness, and simplicity. His good deeds are a testament to the Christ whose name he carried. Saleeb did not merely display a cross tattooed on a wrist, or one hung on a chain around his neck, but he himself sought to be an embodiment of a cross to each person he encountered, exuding love, tolerance, forgiveness and God-given wisdom.

His colleagues verify the fact that Saleeb frequently demonstrated this vigilance and pursuit of purity, even in moments of illness. On one occasion, Saleeb developed acute appendicitis and was in need of an appendectomy. His surgery was carried out in St. Rita's Hospital in Heliopolis, Egypt, and upon discharge, his work colleagues were there to take him home. Exiting through the hospital doors, Saleeb saw an impure sight before him. Though feeling somewhat weak and exhausted, Saleeb made a point to draw the sign of the cross over his eyes, to utter the Jesus Prayer ("Lord Jesus Christ, Son of God, have mercy on me"), and to look to the floor, actively directing his eyes away from the sight which could taint his purity of heart. He toiled to preserve his heart unblemished, unspotted from the world and its vices.

Courtship and Marriage

Soon after his graduation, and as a loving child of God who seeks out the paths of holiness, Saleeb sought after one of the church's youth, the blessed servant Mariam Milad Eskander, to become his life-partner and wife.

His desire to begin a relationship and seek the path of marriage was met with refusal on part of his mother. The refusal was not because of Mariam personally, but rather the general idea alarmed Madame Fayka. As a widow, she required the aid of her son, who she thought would soon return from Cairo to Aswan to manage the lands left by his departed father. In addition, at the time, Saleeb was exceptionally young.

Saleeb's mother managed to also convince Metropolitan Hedra of her position on the subject. Metropolitan Hedra was taken aback by the news, saying that he always thought Saleeb would seek monasticism. "Never agree to this," the metropolitan told her, "and never let him convince you about what's going through his head."

Sister Mariam Milad describes the ensuing events that led to their eventual marriage:

After hearing Metropolitan Hedra's disapproval of the idea as a whole, Saleeb and I took to prayer.

Saleeb related to me that he would travel to Aswan and attempt to convince the metropolitan to agree. The day Saleeb travelled, I prayed much.

On the day he was scheduled to meet Metropolitan Hedra, our church organized a spiritual day which consisted of visiting the monastery in Tamouh.[11] The monastery houses an ancient wonderworking icon of the Holy Virgin St. Mary carrying Christ. The spiritual day began with the celebration of the Divine Liturgy, during which I stood before the icon in tears, asking for the Virgin's help. I entreated her, saying, "O Virgin, please visit Metropolitan Hedra before Saleeb visits him and convince him to agree." I said this knowing that if His Eminence agreed, he would also be able to persuade Saleeb's mother to agree to the idea of us getting married.

One day His Eminence called Madame Fayka and asked her if there were any updates on Saleeb's situation. She replied, "He still insists on it, Your Eminence." She heard him reply, and I'm quoting him exactly, "You will agree, and you will support him until the day he gets married."

His Eminence never revealed what occurred that made him completely and suddenly change his mind about the subject, and since he is known to not reveal such supernatural experiences, I can confidently say that the Holy Virgin Mary visited him and told him to agree.

With such heavenly intervention, Providence revealed

---

11 Ancient Monastery of St. Mercurius in Tamouh, Governorate of Giza, Egypt.

His perfect will: The two were to be joined in the sacrament of holy matrimony. This indeed occurred on Saturday, January 15, 2000.

The metropolitan who once took a stance against the idea of Saleeb and Mariam's marriage ended up leading the ceremony and putting his hand in theirs during the cutting of their wedding cake.

Sister Mariam explains her husband's attitude of placing God before all else as they began their life together:

> I'm going to explain a situation for the youth, something for them to learn.
>
> On our wedding day, I was surprised to find that Saleeb had hung a large icon of Christ the Pantocrator seated on His throne behind the door of our bedroom.
>
> He smiled at me and said, "Come, let's pray together!"
>
> And it was the very first thing we did as soon as we entered the apartment. It was an amazing feeling, and a beautiful scenario. It portrayed how he always prioritized the Lord and kept his thoughts anchored in the heavens.

As a fruitful tree that bears good fruit, the marriage of these two righteous individuals brought forth two wonderful children, Verina and Youstina.

Saleeb Abood Sharobeem and Mariam Milad Eskander unite in the
holy sacrament of matrimony on Saturday, January 15, 2000

"Your wife shall be like a fruitful vine in the very heart of your house, your children like olive plants all around your table" (Psalm 128:3)

Sister Mariam Milad continues:

As a husband, Saleeb possessed wonderful attributes. But in order to be honest, we were a pretty normal couple. We would fight and reconcile. However, we never slept the night of an argument upset at each other.

I really want to reiterate an important point: Saleeb was a normal guy. Like any married couple, we would fight and get irritated at one another. However, the moment he saw my tears, the issue would cease, and we would both calm down and forget the entire ordeal. Let the record show that I don't cry all the time! It was just whenever an issue got serious, the moment he saw my tears, it was as if the problem never happened.

He maintained true humility, one that shows in his deeds, and not solely in his speech. For example, it was humility on his part that he even considered marrying me! I'm a simple woman from a simple town, Al Amiriya, and he was a giant—a man from a big city with a big family, with a father who was a well-known engineer in Aswan, and with relatives in higher class areas in Cairo. To even consider me was an act of humility.

Saleeb allowed me to witness his immense love for everyone around him—never in our life together did I hear him say that he hated someone. Again, my husband was a normal man, capable of being irritated or annoyed, especially in dealing with several difficult people in work or in his service. Regardless, the word, "hate," never escaped his lips—ever.

He was also incredibly modest. He comes from a very wealthy family, but I remember seeing a man dressed in modest clothing the first time I saw him at church. That night I saw a very simple man who did not focus on his outward appearance. Honestly, I first thought he was a poor man! Later I got to know that he came from an incredibly wealthy family, but never gave his external appearance much attention. I remember on several occasions, his mother and I pleaded with him to purchase a new outfit for the feasts, and yet he constantly gave us an excuse; we knew he was content with what he already had.

Getting to know him, I understood him to be very easy-going, not caring about food or drink. Later on, after marriage, I don't recollect that he ever asked me to cook him a particular dish. He was thankful for whatever was placed in front of him. He truly was adorned with virtues.

Saleeb was characterized by a certain degree of asceticism. Again, he didn't care for food or clothing, but he was also satisfied with our living conditions, as well. Our apartment in Al Amiriya was small, and I knew we could afford to live somewhere bigger, yet he was content with anywhere to lay his head. Because of him being extremely busy in the service, he had no time to join me in apartment-searching. I was the one who went with realtors and searched for apartments. I used to become angry with him and fight with him because he left me to search alone.

In all honestly, he told me, "You know, Mariam, I wish to have a beautiful villa—one in heaven! It doesn't matter where I live here." God must have truly given him a beautiful villa in heaven. He loved heaven so much.

Saleeb was so God-oriented that even in our normal conversations, he would quote verses from the Scriptures. We would be talking about anything, and I would find that he mingled verses into the conversation without even trying. Even his manner of speech pointed to his constant attempts to orient himself to the things above.

Expansion of the Service

Like a small seed in fertile ground that produces thirty, sixty, and a hundred-fold, and like a little yeast, causing all the bread to rise, Saleeb's service grew. To compliment the immense development of the hymns service, Saleeb compiled a book called *Rites and Hymns of the Church Fasts and Major Feasts* which he tirelessly worked on. This was done to satisfy the need for a single source in which could be found a large majority of the hymns of various occasions. The book was published and is still being utilized as a hymnological reference.

Saleeb's service progressed beyond the walls of the church of St. Mary in Al Amiriya, and he began establishing services in several parishes in other cities. This included the church of St. Mary and St. Pishoy in Mostorod, where he instituted a weekly youth meeting for the college youth and a hymns class. In Shubra Al Kheima, seeing that a certain church lacked hymnological services altogether, he took a handful of servants from Al Amiriya and handed down the Church hymns to the youth in that church.

Saleeb was chosen to serve in the Bishopric of Youth, under the auspices of their graces Bishop Moussa and Bishop Raphael and aided in the laying down of hymnology examinations and curricula for children, youth and adults of all age ranges and backgrounds throughout the country.

His reputation preceded him; thus, he was chosen to be a senior member of the central committee of "St. Mark's Festival," an annual spiritual competition among several Coptic Orthodox parishes in which over one million children world-wide participate. As head of the hymns committee, Saleeb was responsible for great innovations in the hymnological education division of St. Mark's Festival.

Saleeb became a spiritual guide to all the young men and women he served. His door was always open to offer support in all matters, spiritual or not. He prioritized the salvation of everyone he dealt with and became concerned about the spiritual welfare of all. Many of those ministered to by Saleeb, enamored by the intense desire to be sanctified to the Lord that began to sprout within him, decided to follow in his footsteps; several of these young men joined monasteries as monks, or were ordained as priests. Many young women who learned under him joined convents and churches as nuns and consecrated sisters. Until this day, they consider their vocation to be a result of the fruits of Saleeb's service, regarding themselves as being his spiritual sons and daughters.

CHAPTER TWO

Priesthood and Ministry

Road to the Priesthood

Saleeb's heart was inflamed by the fire of the love of God. He constantly yearned to live a life of full consecration due to his enjoyment of the service in the Holy Altar and the offering of his time to the Lord. He was not content with just offering portions of time, but instead wished to offer his entire life to the service as a sweet savor of incense.

Sister Mariam Milad explains the premonitions she had that concerned Saleeb's future consecration as a presbyter:

> I will narrate a certain incident which occurred that made me feel he was certainly going to become a priest. I was ill; my hand had developed several dark bruises that were extremely painful and sensitive to the touch. I was waiting for Saleeb to return home from work to take me to the doctor. When he came back, I found him incredibly rushed.

He went in to shower quickly, and when he came out, he said, "Mariam, make me a quick meal because I'm in a rush and I need to leave for the Cathedral." He had a meeting with the hymns committee of St. Mark's Festival. I made him the meal, somewhat upset that he wouldn't be able to accompany me for the appointment.

Before he headed out the door of the apartment, I finally voiced what was inside me, "You can't spare some time to take me to the doctor's?"

He turned back and pulled my hand to him and smiled, "Show me your hand."

Saleeb drew the sign of the cross on the area which pained me. He then confidently reassured me: "There is nothing there anymore!"

In a rush, he proceeded down the stairwell. In all honesty, by the time he had exited the apartment building, my hand was completely healed. Every bruise was gone. At that moment, I had realized that God had chosen him for the priesthood, and he would become one of the many wonder-working fathers we know of.

The story of Saleeb's ordination to the priesthood is quite wondrous, and the Lord truly prepared a marvelous plan in regard to how the eventual nomination came about. Saleeb was loved immensely by the congregation of the church of St. Mary in Al Amiriya. Since he had gotten married in 2000, many congregants expressed their opinion that they could certainly see him serving as a priest, especially since the church was in definite need of one. The concept in and of itself was always present before him, and due to this, a desire within him developed.

His coworkers described him as having a specific demeanor: he would sign himself with the cross constantly, he developed a daily habit of reading the Bible before starting his work in the morning, and he spoke softly and offered personal advice and guidance to everyone. Therefore, his coworkers also expressed their feelings that he would make a good priest. He would say, "I want my job to be in full dedication to God, and my entire life to be spent in the church." He knew the popular proverb though—"The priesthood is not sought after, nor is it refused"—so he had kept all of these longings within his heart and as a subject of prayer.

One evening in 2009, His Grace Bishop Macarius, the general bishop of Al Minya and Abu Qurqas, visited the church and officiated the service of Vespers Raising of Incense. Once the service was completed, he asked the congregation to be seated, and stated, "Tonight we will be nominating candidates for the grace of the priesthood. Please write down five names of individuals you would like to nominate, and we will choose the top three individuals whose names appear most frequently."

The votes were organized before the congregation and the results were announced immediately. Once the votes were counted, it was announced that Saleeb Abood Sharobeem received approximately one-hundred-fourteen votes, making him the individual with the second-most votes.

That night, Saleeb and Mariam's phones rang constantly with congratulatory phone calls; the announcement in the church made it official, or so they thought. Two days later, His Grace Bishop Macarius telephoned Saleeb and informed him that he would have to be excluded from this round of ordinations but would certainly be considered for the next round. No reason was given, whatsoever.

Sister Mariam Milad recounts her sentiments at the time:

> Because His Grace did not give any reason concerning why Saleeb's ordination was delayed, this opened the door for several rumors to be spread throughout Al Amiriya. It was a harsh experience for me because I was brought up in Al Amiriya, in this church specifically. When I entered the church, I would find the women whispering to one another while looking at me—many painful instances like this occurred. Even Saleeb would be a target of such instances. Many would tease him and say, "Are you going to leave the church now that the ordination's off?"
>
> Among the rumors that were spread was that Saleeb committed an evil deed back in Aswan, and because the bishop found out about it, he removed his name. The poor man did nothing. At this point I grew incredibly upset, to the point that I asked him to move from Al Amiriya. I could no longer enter the church to pray without finding the women whispering about me. Therefore, we rented an apartment in the Zeitoun district.
>
> He, on the other hand, was given an amazing talent from God. He would tell me, "I won't leave my

ministry, no matter the circumstances." At the time, Saleeb was assigned to minister to the prep-school boys and at the hymns school, so he would insist on going, and would repeatedly meet such disturbing occurrences, and yet he remained committed!

On this subject, I'd like to offer a word to the servants: Many times, we find obstacles that discourage us from wanting to continue in our ministry. I hope you can take Saleeb as an example that you must persevere regardless of the external factors targeting you. A true servant would easily choose the well-being of those he ministers to over his own comfort and relief. It's difficult, but we are called to enter through the narrow gate. Persevere, and you will be victorious.

However, the issue of the priesthood really hurt me, and many times left me crying. When he would see my tears, he would say, "Why are you crying? We did nothing and we never sought out this issue. Why must we cry about it? Whether the ordination went through or not, we should accept it without crying!" He really was unhappy when he'd see me cry about this subject.

But one day, he and I were sitting on the couch and watching a movie together, "Mother Irene[12]—Part 2." There was a scene in the movie where a priest was explaining to Mother Irene that, "A priest receives a direct call from God to serve."

Turning to my left, I saw Saleeb weeping.

---

12 Mother Irene (1936–2006) was the Abbess and Mother Superior of the Convent of St. Mercurius in Old Cairo. She is largely credited for initiating a great revival in the monasticism of women in the Coptic Orthodox Church.

I then whispered, "You always tell me not to cry about the subject of your ordination. Why are you crying now?"

He groaned, "I'm just afraid that His Grace [Bishop Macarius] prayed, and God guided him telling him I'm unfit."

We sat silent.

He sobbed, "I'm afraid that God rejected me."

Saleeb feared that men favored his external appearance, while God may have looked upon his heart in displeasure. This thought, these doubts, upset him more than any rumor or gossip. These instances prove that Saleeb was normal, like any one of us, capable of being targeted with such disquieting fears.

The nominees of the parish in Al Amiriya were ordained to the priesthood on March 3, 2009, and although Saleeb was not included among them, he had hoped that the Lord would look upon his sincere desire to become a consecrated servant, serving the altar and the flock of God in faithfulness.

Years had passed after the initial nomination, and Saleeb was asked to serve as a deacon during the Divine Liturgy which was held every so often in a private chapel. This Liturgy was regularly officiated by His Grace Bishop Cosman, Bishop of North Sinai. Upon getting to know Saleeb, Bishop Cosman prayed constantly as to whether he should nominate him as a candidate for ordination. The bishop developed an immense sense of peace towards the idea and was adamant to ordain the youth who served with him, whom he described to be, "meek, dedicated, and God-fearing." A period of prayer followed.

On the evening of December 4, 2011, Saleeb received a phone call from His Grace Bishop Cosman, notifying him of his nomination as a candidate for the grace of the holy priesthood. "Pack your bags," His Grace excitedly told him, "you're travelling with me to Sinai tomorrow." And so, Saleeb travelled to North Sinai to become acquainted with the atmosphere of what will possibly become the place he and his family would call home. Saleeb joyfully thanked the Lord that his heart's desire was about to be fulfilled.

Sister Mariam Milad describes her experience:

I couldn't travel with Saleeb on the first visit to North Sinai due to the timing of the nomination; it was the beginning of December, and the girls were still in school. My first time in Al Arish was actually the morning of the ordination, after I had officially left my job and completed the process of transferring Verina and Youstina from their schools in Cairo.

Arriving there with him, I immediately noticed an incredible warmth and affection on part of every single person in the church. The process of Saleeb being familiarized with Al Arish also meant Al Arish would be also familiarized with its potential shepherd. He acquainted himself with everyone and grew incredibly close to them.

The congregation immediately adored him.

The family instantly took to prayer, and each member related a wonderful sense of ease regarding the subject. Initial meetings between the bishop and the family were very fruitful. Bishop Cosman asked Mariam if she was in agreement with her husband's ordination, as well as whether she was willing to move from Cairo to North Sinai.

With all confidence, Mariam responded, "I agree, and with the fullest happiness, Your Grace!" Mariam even made the decision to resign from her job and begin serving full-time alongside her husband. Saleeb and his household indeed experienced the greatest gladness throughout the process of the nomination, which confirmed for them the will of God in this next step.

Saleeb then announced the news of his ordination to his mother and siblings. His youngest brother, John, who at the time took a temporary position in Kuwait, was against the ordination completely. John called Saleeb from Kuwait and chided him, "How can you agree to something like this? How could you move with your wife and daughters to such an unstable area? You need to find a way to stop this from happening."

Saleeb responded calmly, "I would love to serve the altar. He called me to serve the altar in Al Arish. How can I put conditions for God as to where He wants me?" In saying so, Saleeb demonstrated a sublime sense of obedience to whatever the Lord planned for him. The area of service was decided—the church of St. Mina in the district of Al Masaeed, city of Al Arish in North Sinai. As for the name with which he would be named post-ordination, Saleeb was asked which saints he took as his intercessors, to which he responded that they were St. Mina the Wonder-worker and St. Pope Kyrillos VI.

The name was decided: Mina. Saleeb also prayed a specific prayer during this period before ordination day, saying, "Lord, make me faithful in the service You have called me to." He felt that the name "Mina" found its roots in the prayer he kept repeating within his heart, since it stems from the Arabic word for "faithful"—*Amin*. It was a pleasant reminder that the Lord heard him.

In a solemn, yet joyful service, led by Bishop Cosman, bishop of the Diocese of North Sinai, and Bishop Kyrillos, bishop and abbot of the Monastery of St. Mina the Wonder-worker in the wilderness of Mariut, Saleeb submitted to the Lord's will. He was adorned with the grace of the Holy Spirit in the sacrament of priesthood, becoming Fr. Mina Abood Sharobeem on the early morning of Saturday, March 3, 2012 at the church of St. George in Al Masaeed. Providence did well to choose that specific date. It was the date Saleeb was to be ordained in Al Amiriya had his nomination continued to completion in 2009.

After the conclusion of the service, Mariam related to her newly ordained husband, "Today's date proves that the Lord never rejected you. Instead, He wished to tell you, 'I merely want you in Al Arish, not Al Amiriya.'"

With Fr. Mina, a blessed servant by the name of Azmy Moussa Ayoub was ordained as Fr. Raphael, who was called to serve the church of St. George in Al Arish.

Ordination of Fr. Mina Abood Sharobeem and Fr. Raphael Moussa Ayoub on Saturday, March 3, 2012 (above); Photo after his ordination (below)

Per the rite, the two newly ordained presbyters were to spend a forty-day retreat at the monastery for silence, contemplation, and, most importantly, to have the rites and rituals of the Divine Liturgy handed down to them. Both Fr. Mina and Fr. Raphael were sent to the Monastery of St. Mina the Wonder-worker in the wilderness of Mariut, and were discipled under the renowned elder, the Very Reverend Hegumen Fr. Raphael Abba Mina, the disciple of St. Pope Kyrillos VI. Fr. Mina raised the Sacrifice and officiated the Divine Liturgy for the first time on Saturday, March 17, 2012.

"Let Your priests be clothed with righteousness" (Psalm 132:9)

Sister Mariam Milad explains a humorous situation that occurred during the forty-day retreat:

At the monastery, Fr. Mina would expect several busloads of his loved ones, those whom he previously served and served with. Sometimes, several buses carrying tens of people each would come to the monastery multiple times a day to meet with Fr. Mina. At the end of each of these visits, Fr. Mina would become exhausted.

At one point, Hegumen Fr. Raphael Abba Mina sent for him to attend one of the lessons to have the Liturgy handed down to him. Fr. Mina apologized to the monk who came to deliver Fr. Raphael Abba Mina's message, telling him he really had to rest and could not attend the session.

The monk then related what he was told to Fr. Raphael Abba Mina, who then responded, "How can he sleep? He must come down immediately!"

So, Fr. Mina got out of bed and went down to attend the session. During the session, Fr. Raphael Abba Mina discovered that Fr. Mina already knew the portion of the Liturgy that was being taught that day—in both Coptic and Arabic! So, Fr. Mina was excused to go take the nap he wanted!

Fr. Mina officiating his first Divine Liturgy under the supervision of Hegumen Fr. Raphael Abba Mina, disciple of St. Pope Kyrillos VI, on March 17, 2012

Ministry in Al Arish

Fr. Mina was ordained as a general priest, meaning his services spanned several areas. He was placed in charge of managing the St. Mina and St. Pope Kyrillos Complex, which contains the dormitories of the Coptic students who pursued their education in the University of Sinai. The complex is found on the grounds of the church of St. Mina in Al Masaeed. Consecrated sisters were responsible for cleanliness of the complex and preparation of its meals, and all reported back to Fr. Mina. He also ministered to the students spiritually, as a guide and father confessor. The students, who left their homes and families, confided in Fr. Mina. He sat with them as they explained their problems, fears, and homesickness. To better minister to them, Fr. Mina even slept at the church.

Sister Mariam Milad relates:

Bishop Cosman told Fr. Mina that he would need to utilize the small room in the church; the youth would awake many times in the middle of the night and search for their spiritual father, in need of him to be by their side constantly.

The room was incredibly narrow, and it contained only two beds and a small kitchen. Many days would go by without Fr. Mina even coming back home at night. We wanted to be together, so all of us managed to go and stay with him in that narrow room.

As uncomfortable as it was, our company together was enough to make us stay in the room for months on end. Fr. Mina would laugh and say, "The room is so small, that the steam from the cooking is filling the entire place!" None of us cared, though. We would wake up every morning to the sound of the church bells ringing; we would emerge from the room with the scent of incense greeting us every morning—we lived in the church! The days we spent living in that room together truly were the greatest days of our lives.

He would gather the students in the complex and pray the twelfth hour of the Holy Agpeya with them before they retired to their rooms for the night. He would sit the youth down around him and engage them in spiritually edifying discussions, allowing them to end their nights with their minds and hearts exalted. Fr. Mina focused on also becoming a friend to each and every student. He took them out to celebrations and outings, even providing them with the means of entertainment and joining them in planning parties, arranging plays and skits, and organizing get-togethers.

He was also appointed as the personal secretary to His Grace Bishop Cosman, delegated to the task of organizing a huge majority of the diocese's paperwork; he tirelessly scanned thousands of documents, allowing the diocese management to go nearly paperless.

"He who sits on the floor shall never fall" (A monastic proverb)

Of course, Fr. Mina's services in hymnological education did not diminish following his consecration. He began instituting deacon choruses throughout almost every church in the entire diocese. In doing this, he began the process of designing a diocese-wide school for hymnological education, with an objective of incorporating thousands of students, who would then be capable to pass down the hymns to several thousand after them. In his words, "I was ordained as a general priest; my job description is to serve and minister to every single church." Additionally, Fr. Mina would praise God and say, "I render thanks to the Lord for granting me my wish of serving His altar. He also granted that I minister as general priest, unconstrained and free to serve as much as I possibly can."

Sister Mariam Milad explains how Fr. Mina connected with the people he served:

> Fr. Mina was unique in that he knew how to talk to everyone in the language they were most comfortable with; he related with everyone. Upper Egyptians have a unique dialect as compared to people in Cairo, and whenever Fr. Mina sat with an Upper Egyptian, he'd switch his dialect and speak like them! With the youth, he'd joke and tease and laugh, and speak to them in the way that they liked. In this manner, he was able to win everyone over, and was loved by all.

Being equipped with a special grace from above, Fr. Mina worked diligently with those who left the church. He befriended the lost sheep and was able to return several young men and women who had been addicted to drugs and alcohol. He personally saw to their rehabilitation and recovery, leading them to the altar to commune of the Holy Mysteries on a very regular basis. He truly took the form of His Savior, who came as a Physician for those who were sick.

Interior Life

Sister Mariam Milad, having been uniquely privy to Fr. Mina's interior spiritual life of prayer and his personal practice of living in the presence of God, shares the following:

> He loved making prostrations and spending long

hours in prayer. He prostrated whenever he got the chance. I would sleep early and wake up at sunrise, but I would find him already awake before me, prostrating himself many, many times. He began to develop callouses on his knuckles due to his numerous prostrations, and I would ask him what the reason for the callouses were. He responded, "My knuckles are just dry."

Fr. Mina was distinctive in that he possessed the gift of tears—they fell continuously in prayer. In almost every Divine Liturgy, he would weep and shed his tears on the altar. In his personal prayers at home, his tears would also fall ceaselessly. One day I asked him, "Personally, I can only cry if I find myself facing many problems. Where do you get all these tears from, Father?"

He replied, "Always remember that the tears you shed are of immense value in the sight of the Lord. In each occasion, remember that every tear you shed is kept for you in His bosom, and that each tear intercedes for you. Tears are so influential in His sight."

Among the many things he taught me, I learned that I must only actively seek to vent my problems, thoughts, doubts, fears, concerns, and anxieties to God. I must not seek out people, since every troubling issue lies within His hand and is resolved by Him alone. He hid anything and everything about his spiritual life and would often seek privacy in anything regarding his prayer life. However, he would still come home in the evening and gather the girls around him. We would read the Bible together, and he would explain the daily readings briefly and simply. On nights when he would come home exhausted from a day of visitations and services, he would lie down and ask me to read our daily readings out loud to him. The girls would have slept by then, and this would be what our readings together consisted of—he would rest, and I would read out loud to him.

In regard to his simplicity, there is a situation that demonstrates this virtue of his. Once, I came back home after shopping for my outfit for the Feast of the Resurrection, and I showed the outfit to Fr. Mina. He looked at me and teased, "Do you really need to buy new feast clothes?"

I replied, teasing him back, "Is it because you're cheap?"

We laughed for a while, and then he answered, "I want you to reach the level of knowing that these things don't really matter. It doesn't matter if we dress in new clothes!" He'd always tell me, "It's always better to remain simple, Mariam." Simplicity was the very language with which Fr. Mina spoke.

There is another incident that demonstrates Fr. Mina's humility and simplicity. He was assigned to pray the Divine Liturgy at the chapel in the diocese headquarters at dawn, from five to seven in the morning. One day, Fr. Mina entered the chapel and did not find a deacon to pray with him, which meant the Liturgy could not be celebrated. Later that day, he and I were sitting together when he called one of his fellow priests, who was in charge of scheduling the deacon services. Fr. Mina kindly requested of him to solidify the assignment of a deacon to attend at the chapel.

The phone was not on speaker, but I heard the priest on the other side of the line yelling at Fr. Mina with complete disrespect. I was very angry, but Fr. Mina did not react. After he hung up, I asked him, "How could you let him talk to you like that? Why didn't you put him in his place?"

He took a deep breath and answered, "Mariam, brush it off. He probably had a bad day, or someone must have upset him." Months later, I discovered that Fr. Mina and the priest in question became the best of friends. It came to a point where this priest would reveal things to Fr. Mina that he wouldn't reveal to anyone else. Had Fr. Mina put him in his place and reproached him months prior, he would not have been able to win him over.

He taught me many things. Once, I was attending the Divine Liturgy and I noticed a woman walking into the church incredibly late. She then proceeded to partake of the Holy Communion at the hands of Fr. Mina. In the car ride back home, I opened the subject up, "Is it because you're a new priest that you're letting people off the hook so easily? You need to be more careful, because so-and-so walked into the church late and you gave her Communion."

He looked at me in a reprimanding manner and whispered, "Mariam, do you know the circumstances of every person? I won't reveal the secrets of this woman, but when you are targeted with a thought about something that does not concern you, tell yourself, 'This is not my business; I should mind my own business.'"

Clergy Perspectives of Fr. Mina

One priest from Al Amiriya relates, "I always used to tell him, 'When I deal with you, I smell the aroma of the saints on you.'"

Another priest from Al Arish describes, "The man was of the age of the youth, and yet possessed the wisdom of the elders."

His Eminence Metropolitan Hedra shares, "When I remember him, I remember him smiling. It was a virtue, in and of itself. That smile, I can attest, has changed the very lives of the people he dealt with here in Aswan."

Relationship with Fr. Raphael Moussa

Sister Mariam Milad describes the friendship between Fr. Mina Abood and Fr. Raphael Moussa:

> Fr. Raphael Moussa Ayoub was originally a servant in Al Arish before priesthood. During his nomination process, Saleeb visited Al Arish with His Grace Bishop Cosman, and had gotten to know Fr. Raphael. They were both ordained to the priesthood on the same day and both spent their forty-day retreat together at the Monastery of St. Mina.
>
> They loved each other and cherished each other's companionship dearly. Either Fr. Raphael was at our house all the time, or we were always at Fr. Raphael's house. Sister Olfat—Fr. Raphael's wife—and I are like sisters.
>
> All of the priests and servants were so loving and welcoming when we first arrived in Al Arish, but Fr. Raphael went above and beyond; he would constantly buy us food, and check and see if we needed groceries or supplies for the apartment—we had just moved to the city, so we were unfamiliar about where anything was. On several occasions, he'd even hire a handy man to fix something at our apartment at his own expense.

"Behold, how good and how pleasant it is for brethren
to dwell together in unity!" (Psalm 133:1)

CHAPTER THREE

Revolution, Revelation, and Martyrdom

A Different Person

Only two weeks preceded the day on which Fr. Mina's blood would be shed, and a visit to Cairo had just concluded. On returning back to Al Arish, Fr. Mina drove the car which also carried Mariam, their daughters, and Mariam's sister. Fr. Mina accelerated to a dangerously high speed.[13] It was nighttime, and the family had just passed the city of Bir Al Abd, approximately forty-five minutes from their home.

The roads, though paved, were hazardously uneven; steep inclines were common, and great caution was to be exercised while driving down this road. It was lined on the

---

13 Sister Mariam laughs and recounts that she and Fr. Mina never agreed on the speed he drove at that night; he insisted that his speed was 120 kilometers per hour (about 75 miles per hour), while his wife insists that he was driving at 140 kilometers per hour (nearly 90 miles per hour).

left and right by a median, separating the road from the desert sands below.

To the horror of each passenger in the vehicle, suddenly an elderly man bent over a cane was seen standing in the middle of the road. The old man glared directly through the windshield of the car rushing toward him, looking deep into the eyes of the young priest driving. His gaze was haunting.

The girls screamed; Mariam and her sister called out to as many saints as they could possibly invoke; Fr. Mina attempted to steer the car clear of the elderly pedestrian who was undoubtedly destined to be struck and killed by his oncoming vehicle. The car lost control, and the steepness of the road did not help. The vehicle slammed into the median, forcing it off a steep incline in the road, and hurling it up into the air and down into the surrounding desert, colliding front-first with a metal pipeline. The front of the car was essentially flattened.

Within minutes, people surrounded the car, expecting to be removing the lifeless bodies of the passengers. Fr. Mina unfastened his seat belt and exited the car completely unscathed, as did his daughters and Mariam's sister. Mariam only suffered minor scratches, some bruises, and facial swelling.

Fr. Mina's first instinct was to search for the elderly man who was almost killed by the collision. He and his family looked around. The elder had mysteriously vanished into thin air. The car was towed to the mechanic nearest their house, and the family was given a ride home.

After the girls had gone to bed, Fr. Mina sat in the living room, staring at the floor. Mariam approached him to comfort him. "Mariam, if we were to die in the accident," he finally expressed, "where would we have gone?"

Her reply was simple and straightforward, "We would've all gone straight to heaven, of course!"

A laugh escaped Fr. Mina, who was still noticeably distraught, "Oh what confidence!"

They both sat in silence.

After a pause, he drew in a deep breath, then sighed, "Tonight, the Lord gave me an opportunity to prepare myself." These words were relayed time and time again to those who came to visit the family after news of the accident spread. The same sigh, the same determined response came, "The Lord gave me an opportunity to prepare myself."

Since that day, an unusual silence fell over the young priest. Before the accident, he would habitually come home after his pastoral visitations and sit with his daughters in his arms, all before the television. After narrowly escaping death from the crash, he instead would typically retreat to his bedroom to read the Bible for hours on end. The time allotted to his prayers increased exponentially. He grew much quieter; calmness allowed his very face to radiate. This novel disposition drew his wife's attention. With each passing day, Mariam began to realize that her husband had become a different person. She knew her husband well, and he was changing.

The June 30 Revolution and its Effect on the Copts

After the stepping down of President Hosni Mubarak during

the Arab Spring of 2011, instability and disarray became rampant. The religiopolitical organization, the Muslim Brotherhood (*al-Ikhwān al-Muslimūn*), founded the Freedom and Justice Party, and intended to enter the June 2012 elections. The party promised to rule the country with a series of policies wholly grounded in Islamic principles, including the establishment of Sharia Law. The head of the Freedom and Justice Party, Mohamed Morsi, entered the presidential race and won the nomination.

With the ultraconservative Islamist Nūr Party coming in second, the Constituent Assembly, now dominated by Islamists, drafted an Islamic fundamentalist-favored constitution on December of 2012, ignoring the participation and perspective of both secularist and Christian members of the assembly.

Political schism was on the rise throughout 2013. Egypt's economy weakened significantly; the nation's citizens grew angry as the rate of inflation and unemployment worsened on an almost daily basis. Attacks daubed with sectarianism were on the rise. There was a clear decline in nationwide security.

Opposition towards the president amplified, leading to the June 30 Revolution, which called for his resignation. On the eve of July 1, General Abdel Fattah al-Sisi, the head of the Egyptian Armed Forces, granted Morsi an ultimatum of forty-eight hours to appease his critics who took to the streets, and who were estimated to be approximately 30 million in number.

On the eve of July 3, General Abdel Fattah el-Sisi announced the temporary suspension of the constitution, and hence the removal of Mohamed Morsi from office. The deposed president and several other Muslim Brotherhood members were placed under arrest. Celebrations by Morsi's opponents overwhelmed the streets of the country.

As he appeared for the first time on national television since the toppling of the Morsi administration, General el-Sisi was joined by several distinguished figures, including His Holiness Pope Tawadros II, Pope of Alexandria and Patriarch of the See of St. Mark. The image of the head of the largest Christian denomination in the Middle East standing alongside the person who facilitated Morsi's demise ignited a common rage among the overthrown president's supporters. And so, pro-Islamists took a vow of vengeance against the nation and its Christians.

Eyes on Sinai's Clergy

As tensions began to rise in the weeks preceding the June 30 Revolution, the clergy members of the Diocese of North Sinai became subject to unprecedented brutality. Fr. Youssef Sobhi, who serves the church of the Holy Family in Rafah, Sinai, relates that priests, especially, faced increasing episodes of harassment and stalking. Besides the relentless hurling of curses and obscenities, a priest was prone to being spat on; a brief walk in the street would render his clerical garment to be covered in spittle from top to bottom.

With the country being a powder keg since the uprising, though, matters escalated: A priest was actively pursued, stopped, and threatened with murder. The cruelty was horrifying. The intimidations, which worsened as time progressed, did not concern Fr. Mina in any way, shape, or form. He was unrelenting in his devotion to the ministry, undaunted by the consequences he fully acknowledged could meet him. Clinging to the vow he took before the altar on the day of his ordination, which tasked him with searching for and returning "the scattered flock of God," the enthusiastic, zealous, and youthful presbyter began to draw the attention of Al Arish's extremist organizations; an onslaught of hostility was imminent.

The Diocese of Sinai's First Martyr

In explaining the threat to Sinai's Christians, it would be amiss to leave out the story of the diocese's first martyr— its own bishop.[14]

Towards the end of 1939, in the city of Girga, in the Sohag Governorate, on the west bank of the Nile River, a young woman a few weeks into her pregnancy witnessed a vision as she slept: an elderly monk drew near to her and remarked joyfully, "The one in your womb is a boy!" When she had come to full term, she brought forth Nabil Riad Gendy on Sunday, May 12, 1940. Hours after the birth, Nabil's mother was fast asleep, when she was abruptly awakened by the sound of the Holy Virgin Mary entering

---

14 The details of several aspects of the life and death of this bishop were confirmed and expounded upon by George Shenouda Bekheit, a personal disciple of His Grace Bishop Makary. Moreover, source material also included a booklet in Arabic printed by a group of servants referred collectively as "Sons of Bishop Makary," bearing the title "Bishop Makary: The Star of the Desert of Sinai," which included a foreword by Bishop Mettaous, Abbot of the Syrian Monastery (a Coptic monastery in Egypt known in Arabic as *Dair al-Surian*).

her room. She was absolutely breathtaking to behold. Light naturally emanated from her raiment, and she stood in magnificent glory, preserving her silence. Nabil laid on his mother's lap, until the Theotokos approached in meekness, gently scooping the newborn in her arms and laying him in her own lap.

"This child," uttered the Blessed Mother of God, "is my son, too."

With each revelation, heaven professed that Nabil was set apart, even in the most calamitous moments. At the age of two, Nabil was struck with a grievously high fever and was at the point of death. His mother, losing all hope, determined to take her dying son to the Monastery of the Great Martyr St. George in Al Balyana.

Her brother, who had strayed from the church, scorned her: "Enough foolishness! What are you going to do there? And what if he dies in your arms while you are there?"

"If he dies in the monastery," she retorted, "I will bury him there!"

She arrived at the monastery, ran into the church, and laid her child before the door of the sanctuary, leaving him there while feverish for the entire night; she slept on the floor next to him.

The clamor of a horse's hooves in the church building roused her. She turned to her son, only to find St. George on horseback, galloping in circles around Nabil.

"He is mine," the martyr affirmed, "he is mine."

He touched Nabil, who instantly fell asleep, as did his mother. When she awoke, she found that Nabil had been cured. Since then, the child took St. George as one of his intercessors.

These supernatural happenings were not strange to the growing Nabil. As a young boy, he would frequently witness doves of light manifesting in the sanctuary whenever he attended the Divine Liturgy. Once, as he approached to commune the Eucharistic bread from the hand of the priest, he was taken aback upon seeing the Lord Jesus standing in full form over the paten.

In his youth, Nabil was an impassioned Sunday School servant, teaching those under him the proper reverence of the liturgy. One morning, he stood in the liturgy surrounded by his Sunday School children. At the moment of the Epiclesis,[15] he instructed the children to prostrate to the floor, and they all obeyed. They observed, though, that their teacher had not knelt with them; he continued standing and was looking keenly into the sanctuary.

After the conclusion of the service, they inquired, "Why didn't you kneel down with us?"

He instantly began to weep. Through his tears, he disclosed in innocence, "I saw drops of blood trickling down from heaven, mingling into the chalice as it sat on the altar."

After completing his Baccalaureate of Civil Engineering at the University of Ain Shams in the summer of 1961, he began working in several cities throughout the country. When given a vacation, Nabil spent retreat in whatever monastery was nearest to the city he worked in at that time. Every abbot who met him tried to convince him to be tonsured in their monastery; Nabil was even assigned a

---

15   This Greek word, which means to summon or invoke, is a liturgical invocation where the clergyman requests that the Holy Spirit descend upon the bread and wine so that they may mysteriously become the Lord's body and blood.

cell in the Monastery of Al Muharraq, where many of his retreats took place.

His first retreat to the Monastery of St. Macarius in the wilderness of Scetis in 1972 marked his encounter with the Very Reverend Fr. Matthew the Poor,[16] whom he took as his spiritual father. Less than a year later, in April of 1973, he departed to the Monastery of St. Macarius, seeking the monastic life; he was tonsured a monk on August 25 of that same year, taking the name Fr. Makary.

Shortly after Fr. Makary's tonsure, his mother travelled to Scetis, eager to see her son. Upon entering the monastery gates, she encountered a painting of St. Macarius the Great.

She marveled, "This is the monk who came to me and told me, 'The one in your womb is a boy!'"

Fr. Makary was described by his fellow monastics as having several talents, including memorization. One monk recounts:

> He would gather us together to read and study the Holy Scriptures. His Bible studies consisted of reading several passages and pages of Scripture at once, and then beginning his personal meditations.
>
> I remember one night, as he was in the middle of a passage, the electricity went out. We assumed the lack of light would mean he would stop speaking. To our surprise, he continued to recite Scripture, going

---

16 Father Matthew the Poor (1919–2006) (translated from his name in Arabic, *Matta El Meskeen*) was a Coptic Orthodox monk who served as a key figure in the revival of Coptic monasticism when he was appointed to the Monastery of St. Macarius the Great in Egypt. After renouncing his material possessions and committing himself to the life of monasticism in 1948, he finally departed this life on June 8, 2006.

on for several pages. When the electricity finally returned, he finally began his meditations. This proved to us that he had a vast majority of the Holy Bible memorized by heart.

He was ordained a hieromonk in April of 1977. He was delegated to serve in the Monastery of St. Mary on Mount Assiut in October of 1979, remaining there for a year and six months. He later took residence in the Monastery of St. Pishoy beginning in November of 1985, discipling many young monastics under him. He was elevated to the rank of hegumen in October of 1995.

A little over a year later, on November 14, 1996, Pope Shenouda III ordained him as a bishop overseeing the lands of Sinai. Upon his arrival to Sinai, a land previously bereft of pastoral and spiritual care, Bishop Makary embarked on establishing dozens of churches. The commitment and enthusiasm of the newly enthroned bishop seemingly provoked local authorities. Bishop Makary was constantly met with obstacles, preventing the furthering of any project he initiated.

The bishop submitted a detailed memorandum dated April 25, 1998 to President Hosni Mubarak, entitled, "A Report on Coptic Churches in New Cities of the Governorates of North and South Sinai." In it, he cited documents explaining every attempted project he oversaw, as well as each false promise and obstacle he was met with on behalf of the local authorities in the cities of Al Tur, Sharm Al Sheikh, Dahab, Nuweiba, Sheikh Zuweid, and Bir Al Abd. Most importantly, it highlighted the need to rebuild the old church of St. George in Al Arish, which had been destroyed during the Six-Day War of 1967.

Hearing nothing but silence from the president, and any other senior official regarding this matter, Bishop Makary took advantage of President Mubarak's visit to Al Arish to inaugurate the military hospital on May 8, 1998. He boldly asked the president verbally to respond to the memorandum sent to him.

The following day, Bishop Makary received a telephone call from the Governor of Sinai, communicating to him a verbal message from President Mubarak. The president asked the bishop to purchase a plot of land in the city of Al Arish, after which the necessary presidential decree to construct the church would be supplied.

The land was bought. The plans were drawn up and sent in. And yet the permit was not issued. The bishop had enough. He purchased a two-floor building in the city of Al Tur, licensed to be used as a cafeteria on the ground floor, and a restaurant on the upper floor. The intention was to develop and use it as church in the future. He began the process of submitting formal requests to the responsible authorities for an official permit.

As soon as Brigadier General Osama Al Marassi, Head of State Security Investigations for South Sinai, learned of the bishop's plans, he ordered the immediate closure of the building. The bishop and those with him were forcefully evicted on the eve of February 28, 2000. Bishop Makary was accused of engaging in religious activity without proper license.

The next day, the bishop submitted a formal complaint to the Public Prosecution Office of South Sinai. He requested a proper inspection of the building, emphasizing that the lack of furniture and equipment in the building would indicate no alleged engagement of religious activity.

In the presence of some government interrogators who were investigating further, His Grace Bishop Makary issued a direct warning to be conveyed to the brigadier general, stating clearly, "The mighty St. George will deal with him as a result of the hindrances he has put in the way of building the church." In a matter of mere days, whether by happenstance or otherwise, painful news would reach Brigadier General Osama Al Marassi; his own son was killed as a result of a horrifying car accident on the highway.

With the increasing tensions between the bishop and the authorities, he knew it was only a matter of time until circumstances would escalate even further. Bishop Makary visited the Monastery of Saint Pishoy on July 20, 2000 and communicated to his brethren the monks that it would be his very last visit. He urged them to be strong and to continue in their struggle for perfection, bidding them farewell.

On July 25, 2000 at 8:00 PM, on the drive back from Cairo to Al Arish, Bishop Makary, who usually remained silent in the car, began to summon the Holy Virgin Mary, Archangel Michael, St. George, St. Mina, and St. Pope Kyrillos VI. His Grace began to stir in his seat, as if to make room for more people entering the vehicle.

He turned to his driver, and finally whispered, "Brother, are you ready?"

The driver questioned, "Ready for what exactly, Your Grace?"

"Man must always be ready," clarified the bishop, "because he does not know the hour of his departure."

"It's way too early for me."

"I love you—you are named after St. George! Do not cling to the world, and let not the world cling to you."

"Your Grace, I would be leaving behind a wife and children," the man mentioned candidly, "I cannot go anywhere."

The bishop responded, "Very well, then. I will leave you to your wife and children—it is time for me to leave." Bishop Makary then asked the driver to audibly pray the Lord's Prayer with him; they both began to pray.

The moment the two of them uttered the word, "Amen," their vehicle was struck by the car of a hired assassin, who waited for them on the road to carry out his deed of killing the bishop. Their vehicle flipped multiple times. The driver immediately lost consciousness, later exiting the vehicle almost unscathed. Bishop Makary's blood poured forth onto the road. He was pronounced dead at the scene of the accident.

Hieromartyr Makary, Bishop of Sinai

Why Fr. Mina?

Sister Mariam Milad pondered the question, "Why Fr. Mina particularly?"

In all honesty, I could not identify exactly what caused Sinai's fundamentalists to turn on Fr. Mina, targeting him explicitly. However, I can theorize how this vehement animosity developed by recalling several scenarios:

Once, Fr. Mina took me to the market to buy some fruits and vegetables, when a man named Mohamed approached us. He explained to Fr. Mina that he was secretly a Christian and received the sacrament of baptism at the hands of Bishop Makary almost two decades prior. He then proceeded to pray the Orthodox Creed in its entirety to prove to us the reliability of his words.

"I've been hiding my faith from my family for all these years so that they do not kill me," he admitted. Mohamed begged for Fr. Mina's aid in helping him flee the country, evading the sure death accompanying the apostasy of the Islamic faith. Indeed, Fr. Mina supported him and facilitated his peaceful escape. This, alone, would be sufficient to provoke Sinai's fanatics against him.

On another occasion, a young woman from Sinai resolved to renounce her Christianity; she decided to run away from home. However, Fr. Mina sought after her and saved her from abandoning the faith. He then returned her to her house after three days of her running away. Could this have aroused the resentment of those who brought about his martyrdom?

I can also speculate that, because of Fr. Mina's position as the personal secretary of the bishop of the Diocese of North Sinai,[17] he became an object of antagonism. Could the terrorists have comprehended the tie between Fr. Mina and His Grace, thus targeting him as a way to retaliate against the hierarchy of the Church?

All of these possibilities come to mind.

With the revolution and its effects on the horizon, Fr. Raphael Moussa invited Fr. Mina and his wife to his apartment to spend the evening together. The priests conversed, as did their wives.

Casually, Fr. Mina divulged that he had been receiving death threats on his cell phone. Fr. Raphael also shared that many of Sinai's priests had been receiving messages and voicemails containing expletives, insults and threats from anonymous phone numbers. What Fr. Mina hid from his wife was the fact that numerous threats were personalized to target him specifically, cursing his Christianity and priesthood, and threatening his life. It became evident that being recognized as a Christian, let alone a priest, in war-torn Sinai, was nothing short of a death sentence.

---

17 Sister Mariam Milad describes that Fr. Mina accompanied His Grace Bishop Cosman on any and all journeys and errands whenever he was in Al Arish. The two were always seen in each other's company.

A Dream of Heaven

Sister Mariam Milad expounds on a vision she saw in her sleep:

Though I'm truly a sinful person, I was granted to witness a wonderful, consoling vision preceding the martyrdom by a few days as a source of consolation from the Lord Christ.

I was sleeping, and suddenly I was taken to a place that looks like a church. In the background, I heard deacons and angels chanting in the most splendid voices. I knew and recognized the hymn everyone was chanting, but I felt as though there was something in my mouth, something like food, that prevented me from chanting along. All I could do was hum. For a lack of better words, I was comforted and peaceful; words fail me when I attempt to describe the emotions I experienced.

I looked around and saw my mother St. Mary, surrounded by many people. I also saw my paternal grandmother.

My grandmother and I spoke much, but I distinctly remember saying happily, "Wow, grandmother, heaven is so beautiful! I truly wonder why people fear death!"

Everyone around me began to walk away, and I started to wake up. I explained the vision to Fr. Mina. With his sense of humor, he joked, "This is so you can learn to stop eating! You couldn't even chant with them because of all the food in your mouth!"

Premonitions

In the early months of 2013, at the first anniversary of his ordination, Fr. Mina accompanied several of his congregants on a day trip to one of the outdoor gardens in Al Masaeed. His family, as well as Fr. Raphael Moussa, also accompanied him. Stories were told, laughs were shared, and spiritual words were given. Memorable pictures and videos were taken that day. In one video, Fr. Mina was asked what his wishes and hopes for the new year were. He wished wonderful things for Mariam and the girls.

"As for me," he openly replied, "in the eleventh hour of the Agpeya, I love the litany in which we beseech the Theotokos St. Mary, and say to her, 'And when my soul departs from my body, attend to me. And defeat the conspiracy of the enemies, and shut the gates of Hades.' May she attend to me when my hour arrives.'"

The response seemed like it was completely unrelated to the question, but mere months would prove the misapprehension of such a thought. Fr. Boules Habib, the priest of the church of St. Mary in Al Amiriya, and the spiritual father of Fr. Mina Abood, explains:

Truly the last few months of his life were full of mystery, and I always possessed a feeling within me that Fr. Mina was selected to become a chosen vessel.

Once, he and I were running an errand to a bank, and we happened to walk by a coffee shop. The smell of coffee could be smelled from across the street. I laughed while telling him, "Fr. Mina, I sense that, just as the aroma of coffee fills this street, the aroma of your holiness will fill the world."

In the last and final days preceding his crowning, Fr. Mina related to me how much Satan assailed him in ways I cannot even begin to explain or utter. I couldn't even bear to hear the words he was saying, or the situations and temptations he was struggling with. The attacks were indescribable; never had I seen a man targeted to such an extent. I wept extensively when he described his final rivalry with the wicked one.

He asked for my guidance.

I was speechless.

Later, I could only produce a sigh and express to him, "Father, like flowers, the Lord is allowing you to be crushed, so that your aroma may emanate to all mankind. We cannot comprehend the reason for this warfare, but what I am confident in is this: The Lord is preparing you for something larger than we can ever imagine."

He beamed at me with his famous smile and said, "Father, I do not deserve such an honor."

Shortly before the martyrdom, Fr. Mina was told that his uncle was confined in the hospital, and the family decided to visit him. The entire family, near and extended, squeezed into the hospital room, as if it was a gathering on a feast day.

Fr. Mina made it a point to pull each of his relatives aside and talk to them privately, leaving each of them with a word of advice he urged them to constantly remember.

He also made it a point to visit his church in Al Amiriya, embracing and kissing everyone he saw in a manner that left them puzzled as to why he was acting so differently.

A certain servant named Ashraf was a close disciple of the late Bishop Makary. Ashraf would organize group trips and busloads of pilgrims to visit Al Arish annually to celebrate the commemoration of the bishop's martyrdom on July 25.

The date was Thursday, July 4, 2013. Fr. Mina received a phone call from Ashraf, who had plans to coordinate the trip's accommodations in the complex on the grounds of St. Mina's church.

"I will book the complex for you. But you'll all come, and you won't find me," Fr. Mina asserted.

In dismay, Ashraf replied, "Will you be travelling to Cairo again, Father?"

He remained silent.

Hearing no answer on part of Fr. Mina, Ashraf reiterated his question.

Again, no answer was given.

At the third attempt of getting an answer out of Fr. Mina, a blunt reply came, "There have been death threats directed to me, so I don't think you will find me here during the feast this year."

Evening had come, and Fr. Mina went to the St. Mina and Pope Kyrillos Complex. He received a request from a certain Sister Mariam, one of the consecrated sisters who are dedicated to serve the complex, to be given the keys to one of the apartments. The consecrated sisters would gather in this apartment to watch the sermons of His Holiness Pope Shenouda III together.

She met Fr. Mina, who beamed with a smile filled with comfort and joy.

"Sister Mariam," he disclosed, "this is going to be the last time you will take the keys from me."

The sister was perturbed, opposing, "I will only take the keys from your hands, Father."

He went on, consoling her, "Don't be upset! But this will be the last time, Sister."

Fr. Mina was noted as capable of being fearful, and prone to panicking at times; his wife had seen him react with these emotions in several instances throughout their marriage. However, since the car accident, it was obvious that he was given a mysterious and wondrous grace of bravery and courage, almost as if the very emotion of fear was fully uprooted.

Sister Mariam Milad relates:

On the evening of Thursday, July 4, he told me that he was planning on celebrating the Divine Liturgy in the church of St. George on the following morning (July 5). The church was situated in downtown, which, at the time, was a furnace of inflamed tensions: violent protests were incredibly common; men blocked off roads with flaming car tires and threw Molotov cocktails at pedestrians and cars driving by. This area was void of all security.

I attempted to reason with him to pray at St. Mina's, which was near our home, far away from all the havoc. In boldness, he answered, "Are we going to fear, Mariam? I want to pray at St. George's, and nothing will stop me!"

In all truth, never in the thirteen years of our marriage have I seen Fr. Mina with such boldness and courage. It was remarkable.

St. George's was the parish in which his ordination took place a year and four months prior; in choosing that parish to pray his last Divine Liturgy on earth, it was definitely a farewell. What was even more extraordinary was his sermon for the Liturgy that morning. I still have his sermon notes; it was a meditation on the verse, "Do not fear therefore; you are of more value than many sparrows" (Lk 12:7). I found that he had inexplicably written: "The Lord counts every drop of our tears, and every drop of our blood, which is shed for the sake of His name, and they shall be compensated a hundred-fold in the heavens."

صح
(لذا) أقول لكم يا أحبائى لا تخافوا :-
+ لا تخف لأننا مسحنا قطيع المسيح الصغير الذى له الوجود الهادئ
+ لا تخف من التجارب لأن السيد أعطانا الغفران (يسلم) (شكراً لله الذى
يقودنا فى موكب نصرته) (٢كو ٢: ١٤)
+ لا تخف من الموت بأى وسيلة لأن مسيحنا كسر شوكته وحوّل
لنا الى فردوس وحياة أبدية .
× هذه هوامش عظمى وتهنئة للمؤمن :-
+ لا تخف من الشيطان فأرب يسوع سحقه على الصليب
+ لا تخف من إنسان والرب معين لى فلا أخاف ماذا يصنعنى إنسان
(عب ١٣: ٦)
+ لا تخف من المستقبل المعتم كل شئ عليه لأنه هو يعتنى بكم أولاً
× المسيح يهتم بالإنسان إهتمام خاص :-
١- خلقته وسلطه على الصليب وكل المخلوقات ذلك ١٩:٢
٢- أ فتديه بعد سقوطه بالأنبياء ثم بنفسه هكبس أحمل رافعاً
الفداء مقدماً له الخلاص
٣- أعطانا روحه (القدوس) بأغالى وثماره ومواهبه .
٤- جعل ملكوته فى ضمنا وعاينّا (عب١)
٥- نحن لنا ملكوتاً سماوياً (رؤ١)
× لماذا يكرم المسيح بنا :-
١- ثلثنا صنعة يديه ٢- لأن أرواحنا نسمة منه
٣- لأنه دفع فينا ثمناً غالياً على (الصليب) (الدم الكريم الذى للإله
المقدس) ٤- لأننا أولاده (السيد يقول ها أنا وأولاده يا أبنائى)
تابع جـ٣
+ يجب علينا أن نثق أن السيد الذى يشمل بعنايته حتى الوصايا
تا تزرع المزن فلا ينساها - صوته شملنا برعايته وعنايته ولم نسقط
حتى لو تخلى الجميع عنا ... وأن السيد الذى يعى من شعور نفوسنا هو
يعى دموعنا ودماءنا التى تسفك من أجل سهله ويعوضنا عنها
أضعافاً مضاعفة فى ملكوت السموات .

The cryptic handwritten sermon notes from Fr. Mina's last Divine Liturgy

85

On Friday, July 5, Fr. Mina celebrated the Divine Liturgy and partook of the Holy Eucharist for the very last time. Afterward, he and Mariam made a stop at the church of St. Mina. He was to follow-up on several matters regarding the complex before he could go home. There he met Sister Mariam, the consecrated sister who took the keys from him the night before. She collected the costs of the students' meals to give to Fr. Mina, who would put the money in the safe. He would then write a receipt.

That afternoon, he sat with her in his office and looked over the accounting records of the kitchen. He collected a sum of money from her per usual. However, she left the office forgetting to receive the receipt.

As she headed out of his office, Fr. Mina called out to her, "Sister, you forgot to take the receipt!"

She looked behind her and replied, "It's okay, Father. I'll just take it from you tomorrow!"

He insisted, "No, come now. I won't be here starting tomorrow."

She inquired, "Will you be leaving out of town tomorrow, Father?"

He avoided her question.

"Just come and take the receipt now," he insisted. "Later on, they may come asking you for the money if there's no receipt to prove that I received it."

She took the receipt, and this would be the last time she would see him alive.

Fr. Mina publicly discusses his premonitions of his
martyrdom on the first anniversary of his ordination

Eve of His Martyrdom

Fr. Mina and Mariam returned from the complex to their apartment at approximately four o'clock in the afternoon. At sunset, the two had a habit of sitting on the balcony, under which grew a night-blooming jasmine tree. With a breeze, a beautiful scent of jasmine would waft right into the balcony, and along with two cups of tea, the evening would be made perfect. That particular evening, though, they limited themselves to the stairs leading to the balcony; gunshots were heard directly below in the streets, and, out of an abundance of caution, the balcony was avoided.

As husband and wife were enjoying each other's company, at around eight o'clock, Fr. Mina's phone rang. He answered, and Mariam witnessed her husband's expression shift from enjoyment to apprehension very quickly. "I'm on my way," he said, "I'll be there shortly."

Mariam inquired of her husband what the issue was, what caused him such sudden unease.

"The military withdrew from in front of the church," he related as he ended the call, "the soldiers are gone." He instantly stood up, telling Mariam that he had to leave for St. Mina's immediately.

Panicked, she replied, "Do you hear the gunshots? How could you possibly leave the house right now?"

Fr. Mina answered with an almost palpable urgency, "The youth in the complex can't be left alone. If there's an attack on the church, I need to be there with them!"

Mariam insisted she and the girls go with him, refusing to leave him alone. As she began to get dressed, Fr. Mina ordered her to stay behind with the girls, who would not be able to tolerate the sounds of the gunshots and explosions outside.

She would not accept her husband's demand, and a dispute between the two commenced. Maher, a church servant who lived directly under the Abood residence, heard the sound of their quarreling and went upstairs, offering to accompany Fr. Mina in an attempt to placate Mariam; she could now stay behind with less trepidation.

With great difficulty, Mariam final conceded, "Mr. Maher, please take care of him!" Maher assured her that he and Fr. Mina would be just fine.

Christians and non-Christians alike were forbidden to walk the streets once darkness fell. Since the ousting of Morsi, Al Masaeed was completely barren of any and all welfare, specifically at night. It was because of this that Mariam was truly terrified for the well-being of her husband.

At the parish, Fr. Mina called his wife every so often to assuage her fears and notify her of his safety. By now, Verina and Youstina had gone to bed, and Mariam was alone. As darkness fell over the city, she phoned her husband once more.

He candidly narrated to her that he is currently stationing himself out in the street, by the wooden kiosk where the soldiers were originally posted.

In complete bewilderment, she questioned, "Why out in the open? Go inside the church and close the metal gate behind you!"

With valor in his voice, he answered, "The men are all sitting outside! You want me to tell them, 'I'm sorry, I'm too scared to sit with you?' It's so that any attacker would leave after realizing that there are people here, that the church isn't vacant."

Mariam ended the call with him and immediately took to social media. She updated her status on Facebook, "Please pray for Fr. Mina. He is currently guarding the church of St. Mina in Al Masaeed."

This status update prompted dozens of family members and relatives to telephone Fr. Mina, one after the other, in order to be reassured that he was well. As he did with Mariam, he also attempted to calm them down, comforting them each individually.

For many of those relatives, this would be the very last time they would hear his voice.

Sister Mariam Milad explains:

The night progressed very slowly. None of the students, servants, or congregants stayed in their rooms in the complex that night; everyone was out in the church's yard.

A young woman among those in the yard began to suffer from severe panic and wept very loudly. Molotov cocktails had begun to be hurled at the church, and this drove the woman to intense anxiety.

Fr. Mina approached her and comforted her. He whispered to her, "Don't cry, you naïve one! It'll just be a few bullets, and then you're ranked in heaven as a martyr!"

Why did he mention bullets, specifically? Why didn't he mention the Molotov cocktails that were being thrown at the church building? Why didn't he mention death by the sword, or anything else? This showed he knew the manner of death with which he would die the very next day!

He then began sermonizing to the youth about the glory of the martyrs, and the wonders that the Lord performs through their bodies—he spoke of things that would specifically happen to his own body later on! He communicated with them about martyrdom with such eagerness and anticipation. Furthermore, all the youth were tense, anxious, depressed, and yet he was smiling, trying to get everyone out of the mood of fear by making them laugh to ease the pressure. It was wondrous that, amidst all the chaos, he endeavored to instill peace among them all.

Fr. Mina returned to the apartment at around fifteen minutes before midnight that night. As soon as he walked in through the door, he embraced me. He whispered wearily, "I want to sleep alone tonight, please."

I instantly agreed, and let him do as he pleased, without debating or questioning, whatsoever.

We had two rooms in the apartment; one was the master bedroom for me and him, and the other was the girls' room, in which were two beds, one for Verina and the other for Youstina. He softly walked into the girls' room [so as not to wake them], spread a blanket on the floor between both beds, and slept there that night.

Morning of His Martyrdom

It was Saturday, July 6, 2013 (corresponding to the Coptic calendar date of Paone 29, 1729 *Anno Martyrum*).[18]

The sounds of the gunshots and blasts progressively quieted down as sunlight began to appear. Silence finally overcame the streets of Al Masaeed. Such stillness proved to be of advantage to the young priest, who was able to fulfill his morning prayer rule in silence before sunrise.

The Apostles' Fast was being observed, but being Saturday, abstinence from food was not kept; a modest breakfast would be consumed early on before the errands of the day were fulfilled. Following a quick shower, a warm cup of tea was leisurely sipped, and homemade pita crackers baked by Om Mina, one of his congregants, were eaten gently as he reclined on the couch.

That simple meal would be his last.

Quietness finally overtook him, the very same quietness which became alien to him last night. Quietness was sorely missed by the priest; his city was devoid of it in recent days. Politics turned North Sinai into a war zone.

None of that mattered now, though.

Fr. Mina breathed slowly, his chest rising and falling with the sedative qualities of a melismatic hymn. His fingers clasped the warmed mug in his hands. He began to fathom

---

18 The Coptic Church still adheres to an ancient Egyptian calendar, which was re-dated to begin the year that the most infamous persecutor of Egyptian Christians—Emperor Diocletian—took the throne (AD 284 according to the Gregorian calendar). For this reason the Coptic calendar year is abbreviated A.M. (for *Anno Martyrum* or "Year of the Martyrs")

how desperate he was for such stillness and solitude.

Solitude was only temporary, though; his Guest had just arrived.

Mariam had just woken up, opening her eyes and recalling that she took the bed to herself last night. She, too, detected the uncommon quietness and attempted to maintain it by walking out of her bedroom delicately.

She sensed her husband in the living room, speaking softly, assuming he was taking a call in a whisper so as to not wake the girls. She kept her distance, now noticing that his phone was not to his ear.

This was no phone call.

Her husband's hushed whispers were whispers of prayer, after all. Something was off, though. This was not the customary manner in which he prayed, and the longer she preserved her position behind a wall to observe, the more she came to the realization that this "prayer" was a two-way dialogue.

Someone was conversing with him.

There were moments where he spoke, and others where he sat and actively listened. Fr. Mina's words were inaudible, but his countenance clearly testified that something supernatural was unfolding before Mariam's eyes.

Her husband's face was shining.

He seemed at ease, serene.

As he spoke, his expressions altered based on what his Visitor was communicating to him. Above every emotion he exhibited, ranging from smiles that would creep in and sit there, or tears that would well up in his eyes, he appeared dependent, reliant on He with whom he discoursed. Undeniably, his Guest would care for everything once the events of the day transpired.

Fr. Mina trusted that it was going to be all right.

Till this day, Mariam never discerned the exact details of what her husband and his Guest spoke about. One thing was clear: She understood that it was the Lord Jesus Himself who spoke to Fr. Mina that fateful morning,[19] telling him that He would care for everything from here on out.

Noticing Mariam emerge from behind the wall, Fr. Mina warmly smiled at her, making it as if no mystical conversation was taking place. Looking at his watch, he realized it was time to leave.

He sipped at the last bit of tea in his mug, finished his crackers, and stood up, prepared to commence the day and embark on his journey to eternal life.

The time was 8:30 AM.

Mariam and the girls usually did not leave him to run his errands alone, especially with the recent circumstances in the city. Today was different, though; upon merely considering the thought of accompanying her husband, Mariam experienced a sudden wave of fatigue. With this unusually abrupt sense of "heaviness," as she labels it, she knew she had to stay behind today. Her fears of the city's condition also limited her from setting foot outside the door. Her apartment chores were not going to do themselves, anyway.

---

19 The details of the Lord Jesus Christ's apparition to Fr. Mina were divulged by Sister Mariam exclusively to the author, and were not recorded by her in other interviews, as far as the author is aware. The author recalls witnessing an almost supernatural level of confidence and faith on the part of Sister Mariam as she recounted this particular narrative and who the Guest was.

Later on, she would realize the fatigue was God-given.

Fr. Mina's keys rattled as he picked them up off the kitchen table, prompting Verina and Youstina to come out of their room, understanding that their father was about to head out for the day.

Sister Mariam Milad explains her final moments with Fr. Mina:

> The image of him standing before me that morning will forever be engraved in my memory; the smallest detail has never escaped me. His keys swayed as they dangled from his fingers. He stood at the threshold of Verina and Youstina's room, looking at me so tenderly.
>
> I told him, "Tell me what your plan for the day is, because I'm seriously worried about you." I asked, even though I knew he never went into details when explaining what his daily schedule was like, and where his whereabouts will be.
>
> He replied, "The car still needs some fixing, so my first stop will be at the mechanic's. Then ..."
>
> And here, he paused. He lingered. He stood silent. All he did was gaze deeply into my eyes in complete silence for several minutes.
>
> What was happening after the stop at the mechanic's? And why was he looking at me like this? Did he want me to go with him? In all our years of marriage, he had never looked at me in such a way. I sensed he was filling his eyes with me. Within moments, I realized what was happening.
>
> This was farewell? My heart ached. I had so many

things to scream at him, so many questions to ask him before he headed out that door. Something precluded me from voicing what I was thinking. An unexplainable power barred me from speaking, from elaborating on the turmoil that was occurring within me at that very moment. At last, the only words I could produce finally escaped, "Okay. God be with you."

We broke eye contact and he quietly walked toward the front door, turning the doorknob and setting his foot outside.

Verina yelled out, sprinting across the apartment with something in her hands, "Dad, you forgot your phone!"

Father grinned at his daughter affectionately, shooing her away with his hand.

I thought to myself, "A priest's phone never parts him. What was happening?!"

His phone was tossed back onto the kitchen table; he wouldn't need it any longer. Upon taking one final look at his daughters, he walked out, and the door closed behind him.

Time to Go Home

The meeting with the mechanic concluded, and Fr. Mina exited the auto repair shop, which was situated by the church. Al Masaeed was more still than the previous day. The July warmth of high noon was dry.

Fr. Mina entered his silver-colored car, and, switching on the ignition, began to make his way down Al Central Street to his next stop—home. A Muslim woman, observing through the window of her apartment, noticed that but a few cars made their way past her building. One silver car came into view, drawing her attention for a few moments. The roaring of a motorcycle startled her, followed by an older Hyundai Verna. The short-lived silence was disturbed by the frantic sounds of a car horn. The motorcycle blockaded the silver car from advancing further, and the Verna enclosed the car on one side, using the median on the other side to further restrict the vehicle's movement.

The driver of the Verna, whose identity was hidden behind a mask, lowered his window, directing a fully automatic firearm at the door of his target's vehicle. Shots were fired, and bullets pierced through the door.

The tan interior was now splattered with blood. A bullet had sliced through the right thigh of the driver. The windshield was covered in holes. The driver's wounded leg hindered his ability to escape, and his attackers now had him trapped.

With the cars now immobile, the Muslim woman watching the unfolding crisis could now make out that the victim of the attack was a Coptic priest. The Islamist pledge of vengeance against the followers of Christ was transpiring before her very eyes.

One after the other, the driver of the motorcycle dismounted, then the driver of the Verna exited his car, slamming the door behind him in a murderous wrath. Each took a hold of their victim's car door and forced it open. Fastening his hand onto Fr. Mina's collar, one of the Islamists heaved him out and threw him to the ground, dragging him across the hot pavement, tearing away the buttons of his cassock and splaying the button holes. His clerical garment was torn with the greatest ease.

He seized Fr. Mina's leather pectoral cross, tightening it around his neck as a makeshift noose, using it to viciously drag him further away from the car. He heartlessly pulled the cross with such force that the skin of Fr. Mina's neck began to bruise and tear.

Blood seeping from his thigh consecrated the sandy pavement below him in a single, elongated smear. Now a distance away from the vehicles, the Islamists sneered, ordering him to stand. In any attempt he took to get to his knees, he was kicked down and stepped on; a shoe print would later be found aggressively pressed into the skin above his heart. The masked fanatics seized a hold of the righteous man from the fabric on his back, which was now sodden in sweat.

They again jerked him up from the neck of his collar, loosening his cassock further, sadistically compelling him to stand upright on his injured leg.

Tears of agony now filled his eyes.

He dangled, wearied between his persecutors' arms,

silent as His Savior who was compelled to carry the wood of the cross. It was the cross with which Fr. Mina was named before his consecration, and the cross he was called to carry in these hallowed moments.

The very same firearm was now thrust against his temple.

Revealing his wicked motive, the gunman ordered wrathfully, "Say the *shahada*!"[20]

Fr. Mina was deprived of any vitality to articulate a full declaration of the Christian faith. He shook his head languidly, refusing their command.

"No."

The gun was then pressed with greater force into the side of his head. The masked assailant looked directly into the priest's fatigued eyes, standing face-to-face with the servant of He who vowed, "He who touches you touches the apple of My eye" (Zech 2:8).

He growled again in a fiercer demonic rage, viciously tightening his grip on Fr. Mina's collar, "Say the *shahada*, and I will have mercy on you!"

With God-given vigor, he prayed, "May the Lord have mercy on me and you."

His fervor daunted his assailants, who stood no match for him. Their only resolution was to pull the trigger. With his firearm, the militant opened fire on Fr. Mina, dispersing ammunition along the length of his body—nine bullets pierced through his flesh.

The first bullet entered just below his left ear, shattering his mandible, and forcing almost every tooth in both arches

---

20 The Muslim profession of faith.

of his mouth to tear free of its anchoring ligaments. The teeth were dislodged out of their sockets and were scattered completely fragmented all across the sand below. Five other bullets were dispersed throughout his neck, and chest and arms. The last three bullets flew through his legs, from his thighs to his feet.

Immediately the priest collapsed.

The intensity of the rounds knocked his blood-soaked crochet cap off of his head. His left cheek was completely blown off, and his blood now hemorrhaged from ten different wounds at once. Steady streams of thick blood ran through his beard and puddled around him. The arid wilderness was now gushing forth with streams of blood, which, rather than terrorizing the Copts of the city, irrigated their faith, and bolstered their confidence.

With each second, his pulses grew slower, weaker. Screams of, *"Allahu Akbar,"* filled the air as one of the cowardly slayers entered Fr. Mina's car and drove away with it. As the accomplices followed the priest's stolen car in their own vehicles, they were all brought to an unanticipated halt a few streets away; Fr. Mina's car suddenly became stuck in the sand. Realizing the futility of their efforts, the killers abandoned the car and fled in their own vehicles, driving off into the mountains surrounding the city.

An employee of the church, Mina Gameel, ran to his parish priest as soon as he heard the echoing gunfire. Fr. Mina dragged himself across the asphalt, spitting out a mixture of blood and tooth fragments. His gasps for air, which were obstructed by the blood seeping down his throat, began to decrease in frequency, and with that, his crawling ceased. With an excruciating struggle he managed to alter his position and lie on his back.

Mina Gameel supported his spiritual father's head, which abruptly turned to the side as if to welcome someone. Fr. Mina rapidly dissociated from his surroundings; it became evident that an apparition was being witnessed in these moments. Turning his head, he welcomed the Mother of his Redeemer, managing to gurgle the words, "O Virgin... O Virgin..." She now came to his side, to attend to him at the moment of repose, as was his holy wish on the anniversary of his ordination.

People swarmed all over him. Some attempted to offer him comfort, getting on their knees and holding his now limp hands—his arms had given out. Others fumbled for their phones, some to call for help, and others to photograph the gruesome scene.

With what he accepted were his last moments, his lips quivered as his final prayers on the earth were being offered. Each consecutive moment was one of torture, of brutal affliction and suffering, but it was all fleeting quickly. What soothed his wounds all the more was the thought that mere seconds separated him from accomplishing his sojourn on the earth, inheriting the kingdom prepared for him before the foundation of the world.[21]

At last, it was time to go home. His body began to go into shock. The smile of a victor, which was mingled with pain, gently materialized on his face.

A final breath escaped. It was noon. A precious crown fashioned specially for martyrs was now his to wear. Fr. Mina Abood Sharobeem—the Hieromartyr.

---

21 Mt 25:34

Hysterical, the Muslim woman who watched the entire attack unfold was now unlocking and opening her window, undoing her hijab. She threw her headscarf down, demanding those encircling the murdered priest to cover his mangled face with her veil.

Several minutes later, an ambulance arrived, and the paramedics carried away the body of the Church's newest martyr. Within the hour, an armed tank carrying soldiers and their superiors arrived, and news cameras filled the street; reporters and radio hosts alike broadcasted a common ominous headline: "A Christian cleric was killed this afternoon after being targeted by gunmen on a motorcycle."

Officers investigating the scene recovered a bloody hand-cross off the ground, exhibiting it to the cameras while pinching it from its handle with two fingers. Cameras surveyed the rest of the site: A silver car's tan interior was soaked in the most priceless blood, and spatters of the same blood colored the sand beneath the cameramen.

The martyr's fellow clergymen rushed to the scene of the murder. Cameras flocked around them; reporters began asking them for a possible motive. One priest declared, "This was an act committed by the deposed president's sympathizers. We the priests carry our shrouds in our cars, ready to die for adhering to the Christian faith, and for supporting our country's freedom."

In reverence, the faithful brought a plastic bag and salvaged the martyr's would-be relics—his shattered teeth. Every single fragment was meticulously sought and retrieved, along with the blood-sand mixture. This bag now contained the very instruments that the Lord God would later use in performing astonishing miracles.

Sister Mariam Milad explains:

I was at the apartment, and I had not yet received news of the incident. I was progressing my way through the chores in the house, only to be interrupted constantly by Fr. Mina's phone ringing.

I would answer to an agitated congregant asking about him, and I would respond that he had gone out and left his phone behind.

"He's probably at church," I assumed.

The amount of successive calls was so great that I would be unable to complete a sentence in one call without finding another call being received on waiting.

Finally, Om Mina's husband called, and I picked up. I could barely hear him; his wife stifled the sounds of his voice by her intense weeping. With difficulty I heard him ask about Fr. Mina, just like all those who preceded him in calling, and I replied, again, that he had gone out and left his phone back at the apartment.

Out of curiosity and worry for his wife, I asked, "Why is Om Mina crying so hard, Abu Mina?"

He replied with tension in his voice, "We heard news that a priest was attacked in Al Arish."

At that moment, I felt as though a dagger had been driven into my heart. I had no way of reaching him and being reassured about him. So, my first instinct was to run to Maher's apartment below me. He and his wife opened for me and I communicated my concern after hearing that a priest had been attacked here in the city.

Maher and his wife looked at one another, then at me.

His wife revealed, "It's him."

"Who is 'him?'" I asked.

"Fr. Mina," they both replied.

I had two phones in my hands, mine and Fr. Mina's. I dropped them both.

I repeatedly screamed, "In the name of the cross!" And I began to strike my face in grief several times.

"Calm down!" I was told. "We heard it was only a bullet in his thigh!"

I started to take my breath, asking them where he was taken, and I was told he was being treated in Al Masaeed General Hospital. Maher quickly called a taxi for the three of us. I sat in the taxi urging myself to be composed when I enter his hospital room. I had to stay collected, I could not cry in front of him when he sees me. I could not fear. I had to be strong before him.

At the door of the hospital, I signed myself with the sign of the cross more times than I could count, and after entering, Maher approached the reception desk, asking for Fr. Mina's room number.

"He's in the morgue," we were told bluntly.

With these words, I felt as though I was detached from the world. My legs could no longer carry me. I lost awareness of all that was around me, and everything went pitch black. The hospital received me in the outpatient clinic, and I began to suffer from a severe asthma attack due to the respiratory sensitivities I have. I was given sedatives and cortisone injections.

When I came to, I extended my arms and grabbed at the hands of all the loving women who came to my aid, asking them if I was in a dream or in reality.

Surprisingly enough, the only thought that my mind could produce was the vision of heaven which I saw, and how I expressed how foolish it was to be fearful of dying and going to such a place. I began to relax and rejoice. I felt slaughtered, yet solaced.

As I slowly regained the ability to walk, my first mission was to walk to the morgue, and I did so very, very slowly. The closer I was to the door, the more rapid my heart started to beat. I began to panic.

Fr. Moisis Naoom, along with every clergy member in Al Arish, came to the hospital to see Fr. Mina and confirm his identity. As I approached, Fr. Moisis, who stood at the morgue's door, realized how feeble and weak I was and immediately slammed the metal door behind him, telling me and those who supported me that he would not permit anyone to enter.

Maher had somehow managed to sneak in, and he exited within a few minutes. In denial, I questioned, "Are you sure it's him, Maher?"

He nodded with dejection.

I fell into a seat next to the morgue's door. It was truly the most difficult day of my life.

The youth whom he loved congested the hospital, filling the area before the morgue. Among them was the young woman whom he returned to Christ, who previously decided to abandon the Christian faith. She threw herself on the floor, before the doors of the morgue, striking her face in lamentation, screaming for her father who never deserted her and her eternal well-being.

A Flood of Comfort

The day at the hospital was just as long as it was painful. The physicians responsible for issuing a burial permit delayed their arrival drastically. Upon persistent inquiry, the priests were told that the physicians feared even approaching the hospital and were not coming. The military had been withdrawn from the premises, and there was fear that the hospital could be attacked due to Fr. Mina's presence. If they wished to have the permits issued, they were told, the body needed to be transferred to the Al Arish Military Hospital.

Finding that the transfer would take a while, the priests advised Mariam to return home to be with her daughters. A car was prepared for her, and she was indeed taken back to her apartment.

Walking through her front door, Mariam disregarded the dozens of people who were there to accompany her girls. God had inspired a single thought to manifest in her head, and she needed to comply, ignoring anything and anyone else; she had to open her Bible and read it, immediately.

As a child, she became accustomed to a certain habit, that any emotion of sadness or anxiety would be met with the opening of the Holy Bible, and she would immediately calm down by a verse that would speak to her. Following her habit, her eyes fell on a verse that drove away the slightest absence of peace: "Assuredly, I say to you, today you will be with Me in Paradise" (Lk 23:43).

Though her tears fell unceasingly, she was comfortable again. She closed her Bible with a novel sense of comfort. Following her readings, another command quietly whispered within her, "Open the cover of the Agpeya." It was in her hands constantly; Fr. Mina and she gathered their children before their prayer corner, using the family Agpeya multiple times a day. Therefore, she had never thought to look in her Agpeya's cover. She had to heed the command, though. Flipping open the cover of the small book, she joyfully wept; Fr. Mina had left her verses from the Scriptures in his own handwriting, which completely crowded the inside of the cover. It was the very first time Mariam had ever seen these handwritten verses, meaning he had to have written them recently: "Do not sorrow, for the joy of the Lord is your strength" (Neh 8:10); "...casting all your care upon Him, for He cares for you" (1 Pet 5:7); "Come to Me, all you who labor and are heavy laden, and I will give you rest" (Mt 11:28).

An additional whisper spoke within her to look for his wedding ring. This thought was especially odd, but like the other commands, she needed to obey. Her first instinct was to open the top drawer of her nightstand, and there it was— Fr. Mina had purposely removed his wedding ring before leaving the apartment that fateful morning. Like his phone, he knew he would no longer need it.

Mariam was overjoyed to see the ring lie there in the drawer before her. In reverence, she picked it up, reminiscing on how it is an object that made direct contact with the Holy Eucharist, which her husband handled with joy on an almost daily basis. The ring was now her newest blessing, and it had to be with her constantly. Attempting to place her husband's ring on top of her own, she found the ring to be too wide to fit on her finger; Fr. Mina's ring could be passed over her own ring with ease, with a voluminous space separating each ring. It would be easily lost. She resolved to place Fr. Mina's ring on her third finger, and she was now satisfied. The blessing of her martyred husband, and of the Body and Blood of the Lord for whom he was martyred, was now on her hand constantly.

Sister Mariam continues:

I was determined to wear his ring with mine on the very same ring finger. I came up with the idea of fastening both rings together using a piece of thread. One morning, upon passing Fr. Mina's ring over my own, I discovered that the voluminous space between both rings had disappeared completely, and that both rings fit securely together like two puzzle pieces—Fr. Mina's over mine. I do not know where the empty space between the two rings had gone.

This is an everlasting condolence to me. Whenever I feel worried, or tired, or upset, or whenever I miss Fr. Mina, I just look at the two wedding rings. I become reassured and overjoyed with them. It is for my own sake that the two wedding rings are stuck together. It is God telling me, "I will never forsake you."

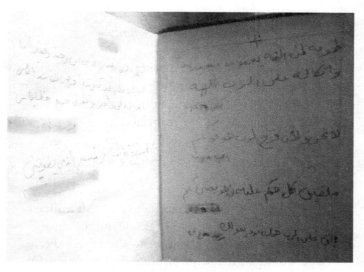

Consoling verses written by Fr. Mina within the cover of his Agpeya

Fr. Mina's wedding ring, which now miraculously
fits securely over his wife's wedding ring

Wonders From the Body

The consolations of heaven permeated the darkness of sorrow. The Lord, who is wondrous in His saints, began to manifest the most remarkable miracles from the body of Hieromartyr Mina Abood Sharobeem.

Fr. Moisis Naoom, priest of the church of St. Mary and Archangel Michael in Al Arish, explains:

By Fr. Mina's prayers, the transfer to Al Arish Military Hospital occurred quickly and easily, and the coroner was able to investigate and write the report. From there we began the steps of preparing the body. Of course, we cared greatly to recover all of the precious garments and belongings present on Fr. Mina's body at the time of the martyrdom. We bid him farewell for the day, and the next morning, Sunday, at 5:00 AM, we—the priests—returned to the hospital with the vestments meant to dress the body. Before dressing him, we needed to bathe the body and clean him of all the blood.

As we started to bathe him, I began to smell something abnormal. This drove me to walk around the entire room to find the source of the smell. I picked up the bags containing the vestments we brought and sniffed the contents inside: nothing. I stood at a distance from the body on the table and smelled: nothing! I did everything to make sure.

One of the priests with me, Fr. Gabriel, inquired as to what I was doing, and I responded that I was starting to smell something, but I wanted to confirm its source. He encouraged me to explain the scent. I described, "It is an aroma of incense, like the incense burned in the censer, but mingled with fragrant oil that is used to anoint the relics of the saints—incense and fragrance!"

He confirmed to me that he was smelling it, as well. We questioned the others who were with us, and they, too, confirmed. Upon approaching the body we were washing, we discovered that the body itself was the source of the beautiful, heavenly aroma.

Sister Mariam Milad further attests to the miraculous fragrance:

The aroma explained by Fr. Moisis accompanied me in every Divine Liturgy I attended from the day of the martyrdom until the Divine Liturgy on the fortieth-day commemoration, especially during the mentioning of Fr. Mina's name with the departed following the Commemoration of the Saints. Even though I have a history of sinus problems and my sense of smell suffers, I can truly attest that once this aroma, which differs from any ordinary incense burned in the censer by the priest, manifests, it is as if my nose is opened. It is an aroma of incense mixed with fragrance, and it has the ability to make people happy; it gladdens their hearts. It is an aroma from heaven.

Fr. Raphael Moussa Ayoub, priest of the church of St. George in Al Arish, explains:

When I entered the hospital, I made my way into the morgue, and upon entering, I opened the casket and saw him; there he was, lying in total serenity, vested in splendor, looking even more glorious than when he was alive. My brother in ordination had now become an intercessor, far above my rank. I took about three or four minutes to weep. I knelt before the trolley carrying his body and stood up to kiss the hands of the Church's newest martyr.

I was surprised to see that Fr. Mina miraculously pulled his hand away as I approached to kiss him! We, the priests, refuse to let our equals in rank kiss our hands, and so, even posthumously, Fr. Mina demonstrated his humility in pulling his hand away, refusing to let me kiss him, though he undoubtedly deserved it.

On the morning of Sunday, July 7, 2013, the priests and Mariam were to carry the casket containing the precious body to the airport; the armed forces had prepared a military aircraft to transport the casket from Sinai to Cairo. As the clergy exited the door of the hospital, a miraculous situation took place.

Sister Mariam Milad explains:

I had not slept for a moment on the night of Saturday, going into Sunday, although I was given sedatives. Due to the situation the previous day, I was in a state of numbness, and I was not fully conscious due to my sleep-deprivation.

As we exited the hospital, following the body of Fr.

Mina, all I recall was that I heard yelling, and words such as, "Freeze," and, "Get down on the ground!" I was not aware of what was happening, and I neither understood, nor cared, nor feared; I told myself that, worst case scenario, I'd be martyred and go to heaven, and there I would see my beloved.

On the third day following the martyrdom, Fr. Moisis explained to us what occurred: At the door of the hospital, exactly three to four meters away, a young man wearing a suicide vest packed with explosives, holding a remote in his hand, stood ready to detonate the vest amidst all of us, including dozens of youth and men of Al Arish, every clergy member in the city, and amidst the body of Fr. Mina. We were all about to be dismembered by that man's vest.

Fr. Moisis, who accompanied the casket, and who took Archangel Michael as a personal intercessor, invoked the intercessions of both the Archangel and the Church's newest martyr, whose blood had just been shed among us. Within mere seconds, special armed forces mysteriously emerged from behind us, aimed their guns at the man's hand, and fired a single shot, forcing the remote out of his hand and onto the ground. They then arrested him.

Fr. Moisis relates that this is a miracle on all counts; the man could have either pushed the button before the remote fell out of his hand, or the bullet could have hit the vest instead of his hand due to any slight movement, causing it to detonate. Truly God protected the body of Fr. Mina and our fathers the priests who were present.

The body was carried on the military aircraft and was peacefully transferred to the hospital in Heliopolis, where it was placed into the mortuary refrigerators. Before the transfer of the body to the church for the funeral, Mariam disclosed to her brother Girgis that the clergy refused to let her see the body back in Al Arish, and that she was now composed enough to see Fr. Mina. She was unaware of whether the funeral would be open-casket or not, thinking that this may be her last chance. Girgis accompanied his sister into the morgue.

Mariam saw her husband for the very first time following the martyrdom. He lay on the trolley before her with an angelic countenance, lying in blissful and holy repose. Mariam tenderly approached her dear husband, whose skin was still soft, and whose eyes had slowly begun to open halfway, revealing his pupils. Seeing her husband's condition, Mariam sensed that he was merely in a state of slumber. Approaching and kissing his cold forehead, she comprehended that heaven was now his home. Mariam exited the morgue and related how Fr. Mina's eyes opened as soon as she entered. Strangely enough, Mina, his brother, confirmed that he personally shut Fr. Mina's eyelids just moments prior to her entrance into the morgue!

Fr. Mina was taken to the cathedral of Archangel Michael in Sheraton, Heliopolis, where the funeral was scheduled to be prayed. Upon arriving to the church, the priests decided to purchase a more ornate casket, one befitting of the body of a holy martyr. The new casket was brought, and the youth were instructed to reverently and carefully transfer the body. As they lifted him out, and to everyone's astonishment, Fr. Mina wondrously began to hemorrhage great amounts of blood, soaking the shirts of the youth; the coroner's examination determined that Fr. Mina had died as a consequence of complete and fatal hemorrhaging, not to mention that this was now the third day following the martyrdom. Whatever blood remained, if any whatsoever, should have been wholly clotted at this point! The same occurred back at Heliopolis Hospital, where a pool of fresh blood seeped out of his wounds and onto the trolley, as though he was still alive.

As the church was being prepared for the funeral, the casket was placed in a hall where Fr. Mina's family was gathered and given their privacy. Fayka, Fr. Mina's mother, just arrived at the church. She approached her martyred son's casket in both grief and veneration. Seeing her son lie before her, she bent herself over him and wept, questioning him as to why he decided to leave her. It appears as though our martyred father desired to sympathize with his mother; tears began to pool under his eyelids, falling in a successive manner down the side of his face! Those present instantly detected the tears, and hastily began to wipe them with handkerchiefs. A photograph of the tears was also taken as a testament to the miraculous occurrence.

Fr. Mina's brother relates that from a medical perspective, the human eye is among the first organs to desiccate following one's decease. For the eye to produce tears three days after decease is physically impossible. To add wonder to wonder, it was discovered that the tears, which now saturated the handkerchiefs, possessed an extraordinary, but familiar, aroma—incense and fragrance.

The transfer of Fr. Mina's body into the new casket; his blood
wondrously seeps three days following his martyrdom

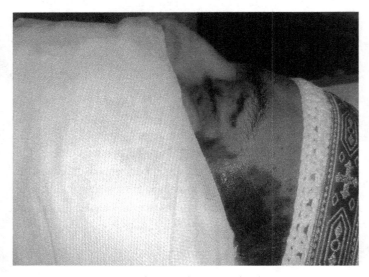

Fragrant tears glisten as they miraculously stream
down the side of Fr. Mina's face

Funeral of a Martyr

On Monday, July 8, 2013, and amidst both ululations of joy and cries of mourning, the casket was carried into the cathedral of Archangel Michael in Sheraton, and the final prayers over the precious body of Fr. Mina Abood Sharobeem commenced. Cameras broadcasted the service internationally. Presiding over the funeral prayers were:

- H.G. Bishop Moussa, general bishop of Youth
- H.G. Bishop Daniel, bishop of the Diocese of Al Maadi
- H.G. Bishop Maximus, bishop of the Diocese of Banha and Quesna of the Monufia Governorate
- H.G. Bishop Raphael, general bishop of the churches of Downtown Cairo
- H.G. Bishop Cosman, bishop of the Diocese of North Sinai.

Dozens of priests, monks, and clergy coming from across the country also participated in the prayers. Thousands of faithful were in attendance. Fr. Mina's pupils from Al Amiriya stood as the chanters of the service, producing the warmest and heaviest tears as they chanted the very hymns they once learned from his lips.

Fr. Mina's youngest brother, John, embraced his nieces as they stood up on the steps of the chorus, overlooking their father's open casket. Neither of the girls wept. Instead, they chanted along prayerfully.

Amidst the environment of sadness, a large Egyptian flag gloriously swayed behind the praying clergy members, soaking in the colors pouring forth from the church's stained-glass windows.

Fr. Mina's skin remained soft and supple, maintaining even his natural complexion. To the touch, the clergy present related that it was as if the man lying before them in the open casket was alive. It was a comforting indication that Fr. Mina truly is alive.

Sister Mariam Milad explains her emotions during her husband's funeral:

> I was given an unexplainable grace from God during the funeral. I didn't know why I stood in the cathedral with the feeling that today was his actual wedding, not the one that took place long ago in the year 2000. Fr. Mina was like a groom walking down the aisle to meet his Bridegroom. I was incredibly happy for him, telling him, "You are now in rest and in full satisfaction. Lucky you!"
>
> Though I was supposed to weep, the tears did not come; I didn't produce a single tear during the entire service. I was genuinely calmed and delighted. I imagined how happy he was, and how happy the ranks of the heavens were to accept him among them. How could I weep as I experienced such feelings?
>
> Before they closed the cover of the casket, I kissed him and whispered to him, "My dear, the apple of my eye, the most valuable one to me! Intercede for Verina and Youstina." It was the last thing I said to him.

Following the funeral services, the blessed body of Fr. Mina Abood was interred in the tomb designated for priests, in the cemetery located on the grounds of the St. Barbara Church Complex, near the St. George subway station in Old Cairo.

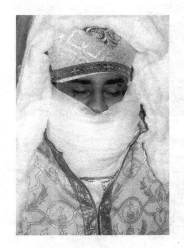 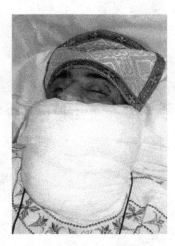

"Their bodies were buried in peace, and their name lives on, from generation to generation" (Sir 44:14)

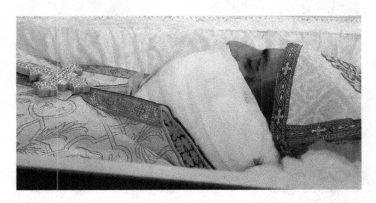

The resting place of Hieromartyr Mina Abood Sharobeem's body

CHAPTER FOUR

Visions and Apparitions

A Vision of Glory

Following the customary prayers offered on the third-day after a person's departure, Fr. Abraam Saad shared the following with Sister Mariam:

> I was fully planning on attending the funeral service, but I was met with certain obstacles that prevented me from attending. Anyways, on the morning of the service, I fell into a state in which I was unable to distinguish whether I was awake or asleep, and I witnessed a vision of Fr. Mina.
>
> He stood before me with an illumined face and a magnificent crown upon his head. He was filled with laughter and delight. A large white cloud covered his entire body, and angels surrounded him from every corner. I asked the angels present, "Why isn't he dressed in his priestly vestments?"

In unison they all pointed to an area next to Fr. Mina, to a folded stack of his vestments. There, sitting in the stack, were his priestly miter, his white tunic, his epitrachelion, and his festive cope. "The vestments are all folded and ready," replied the angels, "and as soon as the prayers in the church are concluded, we will dress him ourselves and lead him in a procession into Paradise."

Dressed in White

Sister Mariam Milad shares the following regarding being adorned in white:

> Ever since I read the words, "Assuredly, I say to you, today you will be with Me in Paradise," on the day of the martyrdom, the burning anguish within me was cooled. I began to comprehend the fact that my beloved now rests in Paradise in the company of the victorious Lord Christ, standing amidst the ranks of the martyrs. My mind went to the verse, "Around the throne were twenty-four thrones, and on the thrones I saw twenty-four elders sitting, clothed in white robes; and they had crowns of gold on their heads" (Rev 4:4). The moment I closed the Bible, I vowed that I would wear white for the rest of my life on earth.
>
> The color white and a sense of tranquility go hand-in-hand. On many occasions, Fr. Mina would visit me dressed in white, so I decided to share in his tranquility and dress in white like him. I remember dressing in black on the day of his ordination so we can match; I'm simply matching him again!

Sister Angele Bassily, the late wife of the saintly Hegumen Fr. Pishoy Kamel,[22] was the first wife of a

---

22 Hegumen Pishoy Kamel (1931–1979) was a Coptic Orthodox priest and servant of the church of St. George in Sporting, Alexandria. He is noted for an incredibly active ministry, and instituted six major parishes in Egypt, as well as parishes in the United States, Europe, and Australia. He reposed in the Lord after battling cancer, which he labeled "the disease of Paradise."

priest who [prominently, in recent memory] dressed in white after her husband's repose. After her, many of us followed.

Though my white clothing is encouraged by the church and clergy, on several occasions, my dressing in white has caused me some difficulties, especially in my place of work. Some people are just not familiar with the disposition that the wife of a martyr should display. In such cases, I would simply explain the reason I am dressed in white: My husband, my other half, is a triumphant martyr in Paradise, and I now dress in white to signify the joy I feel when thinking of the bliss he is in.

If I was ever given the option of breaking my vow so as to escape the hardships that may accompany dressing in white, I would refuse and accept hardship with open arms. It is written, "Better not to vow than to vow and not pay" (Eccl 5:5). I made a vow, and I will fulfill it regardless of the consequences! Besides, the Lord distinguished the rank of widows from many others.

Sister Mariam Milad, wife of Hieromartyr Mina Abood

Father Mina by His Wife's Side

Sister Mariam Milad shares the numerous ways that she felt Fr. Mina's presence accompanying her when she needed him:

> Due to the state of shock I was in immediately after

the incident, I was unable to consume any food. Before leaving the house for the third-day prayers, I suffered from a severe drop in blood pressure. I began to sweat profusely, I couldn't move, and it felt like my soul was about to leave my body. It came to the point that I was planning on calling Fr. Mina's mother to look after my daughters, because it seemed like my time to depart had come.

Youstina approached me, and, being hungry, asked me to cut a piece of watermelon for her. After cutting it, I thought to myself that maybe if I consume a small piece, I would be strengthened. Taking the first bite, I noticed something strange. The watermelon tasted like the blessed aromatic, fragrant spices that are placed on the relics of the saints.[23] I even used my fork to inspect the plate and see if there was anything there. Puzzled, I waited for Youstina's reaction, since she was eating with me. Astonished, Youstina turned to me and said, "Mom, the watermelon tastes like the blessed spices!"

I was suddenly filled with energy and joy, as if I had eaten a turkey! I went to the prayers without the slightest problem. After the prayers were completed, everyone attempted to offer me sandwiches, telling me, "You haven't eaten a thing in days!"

I replied happily, "Today, Fr. Mina prepared breakfast for me!"

---

23 In the Coptic Orthodox rite, veneration of the relics of the martyrs and saints includes placing a mixture of spices and fragrant oil on the reliquary. The spices, traditionally made from pulverized roses, represent the suffering of the righteous—how they were crushed for the sake of godliness. The fragrant oil, which is mixed with the spices, represents the aroma of Christ that emanates as a product of the holy lives they led.

On Thursday, July 11, 2013, I fell seriously ill. I felt as if there was fire within my stomach, and I had absolutely no energy or strength to move. I grabbed Fr. Mina's photograph and expressed, "If you were with me now, my dear, you would've taken me to the doctor's."

At that exact moment, I felt as though an unseen hand had been laid on my head. Then, power began to run through my body, and I was able to get out of bed. I thought within myself to attempt to eat the smallest morsel of food. As I took the first bite and swallowed, I felt as though the food was cooling down every area it came into contact with as it descended down to my stomach. All pain subsided, and I began to eat normally again. Wondrously, the veil that was on top of my head smelled of incense and fragrance, in the area where the unseen hand had been placed.

It was exactly three days before the fortieth-day commemoration of the martyrdom. I had Fr. Mina's cell phone in my hand as I sat next to his mother. I began to flip through the phone, searching for a hymn or spiritual song to listen to. I was shocked to find a file in his phone, which, upon reading its title, forced my body into a tremble. Madame Fayka heard me repeating, "It's impossible! It's impossible!"

This caused her to ask what had happened. I showed her the file, which was titled, "Letter to a Young Widow," a letter written by St. John Chrysostom. Fr. Mina had downloaded the letter from the internet onto his cell phone within a few days immediately before his martyrdom! This is another instance which proves to me that he was readying himself, knowing his martyrdom was coming.

It was written by the saintly patriarch, St. John Chrysostom, to a widow contemporary to his time. It is an incredibly beautiful and deep letter. Truly he is deserving of the title, "Chrysostom," or "Golden-mouthed!" He fully illustrated every emotion I suffered during this time.

I remember that a few days before I read this letter, I was at an office filling out an application, and under marital status, I wrote the word, "widow" for the very first time. It was heartbreaking to write.

I found that Chrysostom had written to me: "I wish first of all to ... prove to you that this name of widow is not a title of calamity but of honor, yes the greatest honor"; and, "that they who have lost their husbands are wedded to Christ in their stead."

Additionally, that if a widow lives in purity, she will, "receive him back again in... splendor outshining the rays of the sun," without separation.

It contained many words that bring joy and comfort. And I advise any widow to search for this letter on Google, "Letter to a Young Widow" by St. John Chrysostom.

Moreover, on one occasion, a group of youth from Al Amiriya came to the apartment to offer their condolences to me and the girls. I still had Fr. Mina's phone with me, and after talking about him and meditating on the glory he was now in, I had an idea to pull out his phone and allow the youth to hear his voice. Fr. Mina saved recordings of himself praying the Liturgies and chanting a few hymns.

As soon as the first recording started to play, we all began to smell a wonderful scent of the strongest incense! We rejoiced greatly at God's comfort to us, and at Fr. Mina's continual presence by our side.

God Cares for the Little Things

Sister Mariam Milad candidly opens up about the following personal anecdote:

I'm going to share my experience with you, though it may be somewhat feminine! After the martyrdom, I took on the example of those who went before me, the wives of the priests who lived in full consecration after their husbands had departed, such as Sister Angele Bassily. Besides dressing in white, she lived her life serving the Church and God's people and lived in the similitude of a nun.

I stood before the icon of Christ one day and vowed, "Lord, after Fr. Mina's martyrdom, I vow to live as a nun! This means I won't care for clothing, since I always wear white, anyways. I won't apply makeup or care for my appearance, or even do my eyebrows! I'll live before You like a man!"

After my prayer, I asked myself, "Will you be able to carry out all the promises you just made? Even your eyebrows? You know very well how hideous they look when they're not shaped!" But just to show you that the Lord cares for the little things, ever since Fr. Mina's martyrdom, my eyebrows naturally stopped growing, and I had no need to shape them ever again.

Believe me, beloved, if anyone would have told me the extent to how the Lord and Fr. Mina would care for me and the girls once he left for heaven, we would not have believed them. There have been many instances in which Fr. Mina was seen actively working and caring for us. He watches out for his daughters and takes responsibility for the smallest things before the big ones! Believe me, it's as if he never left.

Fr. Mina surrounded by his daughters, Verina and Youstina

Father Mina's Teeth Miraculously Seep Blood!

Sister Mariam Milad explains the wonders the Lord performed through the relics collected from Fr. Mina following his martyrdom—namely, his teeth:

> What happened exactly is that after Fr. Mina's martyrdom by approximately two weeks, Fr. Raphael Moussa Ayoub came to visit our home. He produced two plastic bags; one contained an immense amount of Fr. Mina's shattered teeth, which were scattered on the ground after the martyrdom, and in another bag was the blood-sand mixture collected off the ground. The contents of the both bags naturally produced a heavenly fragrance which filled the entire apartment. We were all exceedingly joyful.

Fr. Raphael related to me, "Mr. Ibrahim, who owns a plumbing tools shop directly in front of where the incident took place, collected every fragment of the teeth and the blood-sand mixture." He proceeded to give us three little fragments of the broken teeth—one piece for me, one for Verina, and one for Youstina. Another fragment was given to me to give to Fr. Mina's mother. The rest of the bag with all its blessed contents was given to His Grace Bishop Cosman, bishop of North Sinai.

We were also given a small amount of the blessed blood-sand mixture. I brought a small plastic bag to place the sand in, but I could not find another one for the fragments of the teeth—it was all part of God's plan. "We do not need a bag," Fr. Raphael said, pulling tissues out of a box before him. "We can wrap them in these." Fr. Raphael enveloped the fragments in the tissues and placed the bag of sand and the teeth in a wooden tube reliquary. "No one is to open the reliquary," he ordered as he sealed the tube shut with a nail and screwdriver. "Whoever wants to take a blessing can do so by touching the outside of the tube."

A few months later, in November of 2013, Fr. Lukas, priest of the church of St. Luke in Old Cairo, came to visit us, requesting to take a small blessing from the relics for his parish. He opened the tube and immediately we were greeted with a wonderful scent of heavenly fragrance! We all rejoiced and chanted the hymn, "Axios," over and over again. What was greater is that, in the tube, we noticed that the white tissues in which Fr. Raphael had wrapped the relics were folded separately beside the fragments and had now become soaked in fresh blood—blood that seems like it had trickled only hours before! This was the first time Fr. Mina's teeth bled.

Later, His Grace Bishop Cosman came to visit us, as was his custom every so often. I explained what happened in regard to the teeth and the blood that miraculously seeped from them.

"Hand me a screwdriver," he told me. We opened the reliquary tube again, and he removed the blood-soaked tissues and examined them himself. "Thank you very much," he laughed as he folded the tissues and placed them in the chest pocket of his cassock.

I was admittedly disappointed, but His Grace, in his fatherhood and compassion, comforted me, "Do not be upset! This is so we can place it in Fr. Mina's shrine!" He wrapped the fragments of teeth into new tissues and placed them again into the reliquary tube.

Anyways, my beloved husband did not wish to leave me upset. God brought me a deacon, who was sent on behalf of His Grace Bishop Ermia, to take a blessing of the relics for the Shrine of the Contemporary Martyrs in the Coptic Orthodox Cultural Center on the grounds of St. Mark's Cathedral in Al Abbasiya. We unsealed the reliquary once more, and, to my surprise, the new tissues were soaked in much, much more blood than the previous tissues taken by Bishop Cosman! Fr. Mina wished to gladden my heart! This time, though, I resolved within myself that I would remain silent so as to not have these taken away from me as well.

However, I'm unable to keep quiet, and I revealed the miracle again. The tissues were cut into pieces and distributed among the clergy until I was left with two of the smallest pieces of the blood-soaked tissues!

The reliquary containing the precious relics of Hieromartyr Mina Abood in the home of Sister Mariam Milad

Father Mina's Visits

Sister Mariam Milad explains her husband's visits to her following his martyrdom:

Fr. Mina used to visit me many times during the period of time immediately following his martyrdom.

When I would arise from my sleep, I would tell of the conversations he and I had. People began to assume it was my subconscious thoughts which produced these dreams.

However, to prove the validity of the visions, he once paid a visit to Fr. Moisis Naoom in a vision. Greeting Fr. Moisis, Fr. Mina whispered, "Send my regards to Mariam, and say hello to Verina and Youstina for me!" Fr. Moisis, arising from his sleep, then telephoned me and delivered the message. I was overjoyed. After a while, these dreams began to decrease in frequency, and had pretty much ceased altogether.

It came to the point that I thought to myself, "Have I become evil, and unworthy of his visits? Is he angry with me?" Hence, I made a phone call to Sister Angele Bassily. I communicated my concerns to her. She empathized with me, saying, "Fr. Pishoy would visit me very often immediately after his departure, as well. As time passed, I, too, found that the visits decreased in frequency. These saintly fathers, after taking permission from the Lord, come to visit us very often in the beginning to strengthen us. Once they find us toughened and composed enough, they begin focusing on their service to all men."

Once, it was the night of Fr. Mina's birthday, and I hadn't seen Fr. Mina in a long time. After my prayers were completed, I stood and complained to the Lord, saying, "Lord, today is his birthday! I wish to see him! Please, Lord, allow me to see Fr. Mina tonight."

I fell asleep, and I saw the following vision:

Fr. Mina approached me, chuckling and teasing,

"Are you still whining like you used to do?"

I replied, laughing, "Well, what am I to do? I want you to come visit me every day!"

He replied that he could not do so anymore, since he has more services he is in need of fulfilling now. A beautiful conversation between us began. Though the visits decreased in frequency, he constantly tells me that he is with us, by our side, and has never left us.

Every single time he comes, he greets me with the words "I'm alive."

Once, he came to visit me, and I asked him, "Where are you staying now?"

He joyfully responded, "I'm staying with the angels and saints in the glories of heaven."

Father Raphael Moussa's Premonitions

Sister Mariam Milad tells of the visit of Fr. Raphael Moussa Ayoub, and the mysterious words he expressed to her that evening:

I'm going to explain a situation that occurred with Fr. Raphael, one which I will never forget. Fr. Raphael came to the apartment to offer his condolences to us. A few hours into the visit, he quietly took me aside, away from everyone, and whispered, "I want you to consider the words I am about to tell you as if they're words of confession—do not divulge anything I am about to say until later."

I told him to proceed.

He calmly revealed, "What happened to Fr. Mina is going to happen to me—exactly: I will die the same death with which Fr. Mina died."

I initially thought he said these words to try to comfort me. I quickly realized that he was serious. Agitated, I responded, "No, Father! May God preserve your life and keep your priesthood. Don't say that!"

He then smiled and replied, "You will see! It will happen, and you'll say, 'Fr. Raphael said so.'"

On June 30, 2016, almost exactly three years later, Fr. Raphael Moussa Ayoub was getting his car fixed at the mechanic when a masked individual, who stalked him from the start of the day, snuck behind him. This man, an ISIS militant, then drew a gun and fired a shot into Fr. Raphael's shoulder. Our father yelled, "O Lord!"

Next, another shot was fired at the back of his head. He fell to the ground and spread his arms out in the form of a cross. Thus, he gained the crown of martyrdom through the exact same method as Fr. Mina.

I realized that this wasn't the hand of terrorism at play, or an evil plot that was organized by terrorists. It was truly a divine plan that was even revealed beforehand to this martyred father, a plan he had actually agreed to; he knew about the exact scenario years before it had occurred, even the method with which he would be martyred! Fr. Raphael was even surrounded by several other Christians at the time, yet it wasn't a massacre—he was the only one killed! I truly felt that God was more powerful than the terrorists, far above the capabilities and comprehension of the militants responsible; He has a specific plan that surpasses our understanding; truly He is the Pantocrator.

Hieromartyr Raphael Moussa Ayoub

CHAPTER FIVE

Anecdotes, Miracles, and Commemoration

Short Anecdotes

Saleeb demonstrated his wisdom in dealing with the youth. He was once asked to deliver a sermon about martyrdom on the eve of the Coptic New Year.[24] Upon completion of the sermon, he asked one of the youth in attendance, "Where would you like to end up once your life here concludes?"

The youth joked, "Wherever there are girls!"

Saleeb laughed, "There are girls in both places!"

The youth responded, "Then I'll go where the girls are more beautiful."

Saleeb answered, "The beauty of the girls in heaven,

---

24 According to the Coptic calendar, the Coptic New Year falls on the corresponding Gregorian calendar date of September 11th (or September 12th if the previous Coptic year was a leap year).

[such as Sts. Marina, Demiana, and Barbara] is of a different kind! But I don't believe that's what you have in mind."

Mrs. Engy Magdy recounts:

> Fr. Mina was my hymns teacher in the church of St. Mary in Al Amiriya. I have to say that, even as a layman, Fr. Mina (then Saleeb) demonstrated that he possessed a gift of clairvoyance and knowing hidden matters.
>
> I was about to get engaged, and, besides my close family members, no one knew about the relationship I was in. Considering Saleeb as one of my spiritual guides, I decided within myself to approach him and notify him of the news.
>
> As I advanced towards him, before I spoke a word, he exclaimed, "Congratulations!"
>
> To say I was confused would be an understatement. I stood before him speechless for several minutes.
>
> He reiterated, "Congratulations, dear! Who's the groom?"
>
> I questioned him as to how he could have possibly known, since no one else had been notified!
>
> He chuckled, "I was made aware—that's all I will say."
>
> Requesting details, I found that he immediately changed the subject and avoided my questions.

Whenever Saleeb taught hymns to a group of youth, he would usually have them seated as they learned.

When it was time for them to repeat after him, he would say, "Kindly, rest."

Though this phrase in Arabic is meant to be said when asking someone to be seated, he would say this to signal to the youth that it was time to stand up and chant! The youth before him would laugh, and Saleeb would remind them that in chanting the hymns, the language of the heavenly, one truly finds rest.

Saleeb was always sought after for advice by the youth in his church. Many times, they would sit before him and weep when explaining the difficulties they faced.

Saleeb would comfort them and say, "These problems don't deserve your tears. Your tears should be saved for your prayers! Everything else is trivial in comparison."

Fr. Youssef Sobhi sustained a severe injury in his leg and yet insisted that the injury would not hinder him from praying the Divine Liturgy the very next day. The next morning came and he could not pray.

Fr. Youssef called Fr. Mina, asking him to celebrate the Divine Liturgy in his place, telling him about the injury he sustained.

To his surprise, Fr. Youssef found that Fr. Mina came to visit him very early that morning before heading to the church. He wished to be reassured about him. Fr. Mina even made it a point to visit him daily and change the bandages himself.

Fr. Mina was characterized as having a constant reliance on the Lord his God. One of his famous sayings, which he said in times of tribulation, included, "Our God sees, our God hears; our God will deal with it."

Fr. Mina developed a habit of offering a prostration to his congregants, whether he upset them or not. One always found the spirit of humility in him.

His daughter, Youstina, relates that he advised her to pray, at the very least, once in the morning and once at night. He told her not to focus solely on the recitation of the words, but to express them in such a way as to initiate a dialogue with her Lord.

Nancy Boutros, a servant from Al Arish, explains:

I began my interaction with Fr. Mina when I first moved to Al Arish on March 19, 2013. My husband had just passed away, after the departure of my father by merely six months. I began to serve with Fr. Mina while coping with the loss of my loved ones.

At one point, I was in emotional turmoil due to the successive departures of my mother, then my father, then my husband.

He knocked on the door of my office, entering and finding me in this condition.

He comforted me, "I'm not that much older than you, daughter. However, from this day, consider me as being the one responsible for you."

I felt as though he sensed every emotion within me, without a word being said on my part. Till this day, whenever I am faced with a problem, I call upon him and remind him that he took responsibility over me. Never has he let me down.

On another occasion, I was working on the computer in the office when the internet connection was lost. I began to remember my husband, who always knew how to repair the internet connection, and I began to tear up. At this moment, Fr. Mina knocked and entered. I attempted to appear strong in front of him, hiding my tears.

He smiled and asked, "I hope the internet

connection is working! I have an urgent e-mail I need to send out."

I couldn't believe what he said. I explained the problem, making sure not to appear weak before him.

In compassion, he replied, "Daughter, do not be upset anymore. The Lord shall 'send you help from His sanctuary'" (Ps 20:2).

Truly he was deserving of the crown of martyrdom due to his kindheartedness, compassionately giving himself to others, until ultimately he gave his life to God

Various Miracles Attributed to Father Mina

A servant from the church of St. Mary in Al Amiriya shares the following experience:

> During Fr. Mina's last visit to Al Amiriya, he asked me about one of the girls he used to serve while he was here. I related to him that she was in need of deep prayers; she and her husband attempted many times to conceive, and yet they could not. Their doctors also told them that there was little to no chance of conception, and it left them in a state of constant sadness.
>
> He smiled at me and promised, "No, do not worry. Very soon she will bear a beautiful little baby."
>
> Within mere days of Fr. Mina's travelling to Paradise, I received news that she had become pregnant.

Sister Mariam Milad narrates:

> I have a coworker by the name of Emad who had previously suffered from severe stomach aches. His physician prescribed him with a medication that eased his pains completely. A long period of time passed, and he was without pain, thankfully.
>
> Unexpectedly, one day, the stomach pains

returned. Forgetting the name of the medication he took, he attempted to look for the prescription he previously received in order to get more medication. He looked for the paper all over his apartment and could not find it.

As he was looking, he found a photo of Fr. Mina, which I gave him, and he spoke to him, saying, "Father, your wife is a coworker of mine. Please direct me to the name of the medication, because I am in serious pain."

That night, he placed the photo of Fr. Mina on the pillow next to him and slept. When he awoke, next to the photo, he found a folded-up white piece of paper. Unfolding it, he found the name of the medication written in Fr. Mina's handwriting!

Sister Mariam Milad also recounts:

A young woman by the name of Marihan, originally one of the students whom Fr. Mina taught in the hymns school, was about to deliver her child prematurely. The night before the delivery, her physician administered another ultrasound and revealed that the child would be born weighing only 1.3 kilograms with underdeveloped lungs. He would need to be placed in an incubator post-birth. Throughout the night, she asked for Fr. Mina's prayers on her behalf, and on behalf of her unborn son.

The next morning, before she was taken into the delivery room, she placed a photo of Fr. Mina under her surgical hairnet. Being conscious during the entire delivery process, Marihan described that she suddenly saw Fr. Mina standing beside her nurses, smiling at her and easing her worry.

The child was born healthy, weighing 2.6 kilograms, and with fully developed lungs. He doubled in weight overnight! Physicians deemed that it was no longer necessary to place the newborn in an incubator.

Marihan brought me the ultrasound taken before birth and the birth certificate which recorded his new weight, showing me how the Lord became glorified by the prayers of His valued martyr, Fr. Mina Abood Sharobeem.

Sister Mariam Milad explains the following miracle:

Fr. Mina's miracles are without number. He truly is very active and works for the glory of God. Recently, I received a phone call from a woman who explained to me how she suffered a stroke which led to hemiparalysis: one of her arms and one of her legs became paralyzed, as did half of her face. Being a mother of several young children, many came to her recommending that she ask for the prayers of Fr. Mina Abood, who developed a reputation of being an incredible wonder-worker.

In tears, she entreated to him, "Fr. Mina, all I ask is that I am able to stand up again so I may be able to serve my children."

Indeed, Fr. Mina appeared to her dressed in his beautiful liturgical vestments, with a cross in his hand. He only looked at her and smiled. She described him as possessing an aura of splendor and holiness, and his face shone greatly.

Suddenly, she was able to move her arm, then her leg followed immediately. Her facial paralysis also subsided, and she stood up within minutes of witnessing the vision.

Mr. N. G. explains:

In May of 2016, I suffered a massive stroke and was transferred to the intensive care unit at Al Hayat Hospital in Heliopolis. There, I requested the cap worn by Fr. Mina Abood. I wore it on my head and invoked the prayers of the martyr and his intercessions so that the Lord may grant me healing. Indeed, the stroke was completely healed without any medical intervention whatsoever. Though my physicians communicated that I would deal with lifetime effects, I was discharged from the hospital without suffering any consequences of the stroke.

D. N. recounts:

I underwent LASIK eye surgery, which is known to leave a temporary side effect of dry eyes, increasing due to hot weather. However, my doctor related that the side effects I suffered were much more severe and long-term due to certain complications. Tears were not being produced at all. This meant that I began to develop accumulations of dust particles along the edges of my eye lashes.

Over time, I had an infection in my eyelids, leaving deposits of oily sacs. I underwent two procedures to remove these deposits, and they were incredibly painful; I felt the scalpel being used by the physician to drain these deposits. The last procedure of this kind occurred in December of 2014.

I paid a visit to Sister Mariam Milad, the wife of Fr. Mina Abood, in her apartment in January of 2015. She gave me a small piece of cotton that was placed on the body of Fr. Mina after his martyrdom, and I placed the cotton on my eye.

Immediately, I felt as though all dryness had ceased, and my eye became lubricated once more. In the beginning, I assessed that the lack of dryness was due to a lack in the hot weather, since it was winter at the time. I told myself that if the summer season arrives without me sensing any dryness, then it was truly a miracle performed through the prayers of Fr.

Mina. Indeed, the summer season arrived, and it was one of the hottest and driest summers on record. I did not feel any dryness in either eye. I forgot the whole ordeal.

However, one day, specifically in October of 2015, another deposit formed in my eyelid and the dryness returned. I remembered the piece of cotton I took from Sister Mariam, and I placed it on my eye, saying, "If the deposit disappears, then this confirms the miracle I had forgotten about, and I will telephone Sister Mariam and notify her."

As I removed the piece of cotton off my eye, I discovered that the oily deposit had disappeared, though surgical intervention was needed to drain and remove it. I immediately called Sister Mariam, notifying her that the Lord wrought a miracle through the prayers of Fr. Mina Abood Sharobeem.

A youth from the United States relates:

I am a graduate student. One of the courses I was enrolled in was known to be taught by a professor notorious for complicating her exams. Two exams comprised the entire course grade: a midterm exam and a final exam. I required a course average of 70.0% to pass the class and avoid the course remediation exam, which is cumulative in format, including all the material from the entire semester. Failing the remediation requires repetition of the entire year. This course was known as being one of those courses where a miracle is needed to pass.

After studying for over two weeks straight, night and day, I entered the auditorium to write the final exam. An empty seat was to be left between one student and the other, so I called on Fr. Mina Abood to come and sit next to me, guiding me to my answers. I wrote the exam and found that it was incredibly difficult. I seriously doubted that I had passed the class.

About a week later, I was attending an evening Divine Liturgy during the Great Fast. After the Liturgy, I received dozens of messages from my classmates, telling me that the final grades were released. Still being in church, I immediately made my way to the Sanctuary, and placed my cell phone on the Altar before checking my grade there. I called on Fr. Mina once more, and I was confident that I had passed.

Opening my grade on the Altar, I found that my course average was 69.8%, and was miraculously rounded up to 70.0%! Every student needs to know that Fr. Mina is an incredible intercessor and friend, gladdening the hearts of all those who call upon him.

Glory to God in His saints. Amen.

The same youth also recounts:

A relative of mine suffered from alarming symptoms, including severe fatigue and violent coughing episodes. He travelled to Cairo to be examined, and it was revealed that my relative, who was recently married, had lung cancer.

Later, he developed several new symptoms, including yellowing of the skin and numbness in his extremities. It was now revealed that his cancer had metastasized [i.e., spread] to his lymph nodes. The diagnosis was confirmed by three different oncologists, including one who previously diagnosed a family member of his with cancer who ended up passing away as a result. With the cancer confirmed by the three physicians, a biopsy was needed to just confirm staging. Metastasis meant the cancer was at least stage three.

At the same time, his wife was diagnosed with a severe ovarian cyst. She previously had a similar cyst and half of her ovary was surgically removed. Removal of this new cyst could render her infertile, and lack of removal could cause the cyst to rupture, which would be life-threatening.

I instructed both of them to ask for the prayers of Hieromartyr Mina Abood. I also placed their names under a reliquary containing the blood of Fr. Mina, that God may interfere and heal this man and his wife, who were just beginning their lives together.

Both the cyst surgery and the biopsy procedure were scheduled to be on the same day. When the results of the biopsy came in, each of the three oncologists were perplexed. The biopsy came back negative. The tissue was found not to be cancerous at all but was rather produced as a result of an autoimmune condition. The physicians were stunned, since the symptoms he displayed did not match the autoimmune condition that the biopsy confirmed. The oncologists stated that they had never seen anything like this in their respective medical careers, especially since cancer was confirmed without a single doubt. His symptoms wondrously subsided also, and he is now in good health.

As for his wife, the cyst was removed miraculously, and her fertility was in no way affected. The newlyweds both glorified the Lord, who is wondrous in His saints, and in His chosen martyr, Fr. Mina Abood Sharobeem.

Mrs. Mona Girgis Ramzy describes her wondrous experience:

I knew Fr. Mina before he was a priest, and I knew Sister Mariam well; we were good friends. When they travelled to Al Arish, we pretty much lost contact. Though he moved, Fr. Mina telephoned me several times to ask about me. His voice was so calming. When he was martyred, I mourned greatly, but I was also comforted at the fact that I had an acquaintance who became a martyr. Since then, I had not called on him or asked for his prayers at any particular point.

In February of 2016, I grew incredibly ill. I was

taken to Al Salam Hospital in Al Mohandessin and the physicians ran their tests. My systolic blood pressure measured 185 mm Hg. Three days into my stay at the hospital, my exhaustion reached a record. Though I was completely dehydrated and drank huge amounts of water, ultrasound imaging detected that my bladder was completely empty. My feet and hands swelled, and I was told that I suffered from acute renal failure. Later that day, I fell into a coma. My family was told that within a day or so I would be dead.

In my coma, I witnessed a vision. I found myself in a room with white walls, and Fr. Mina appeared before me. He gave me the purest smile, just as he is pictured in his photos. He said nothing to me, but the look on his face reassured me that I would recuperate and live, for the glory of God's name. At that moment, I opened my eyes.

When I awoke, the first thing I heard was one of the nurses screaming, "Doctor! Her kidneys are functioning again!"

I found myself wearing an article of Fr. Mina's liturgical vestments—one of the altar socks he used to wear during the Divine Liturgy. Sister Mariam brought it to me and put it on my foot while I was in my coma.

The more I became conscious of my surroundings, the more I began to realize that I was covered in tubes and wires. I asked the doctors, among whom was Dr. Maher Asaad, the renowned nephrologist, to let me get up out of bed and move again.

The doctor responded, "You cannot move. The only thing you can, and should, do is talk to the Lord and thank Him for saving you from what happened to you."

I was told that, as a consequence to both my kidneys failing, I developed severe uremia, and the amount of waste material in my blood showed I would never live to see another day. My lungs became infected. I developed a stroke. All of this occurred, and yet as soon as I awoke from the coma, all of these conditions miraculously vanished. Within days, I was discharged, and I am now in good health by the many graces of God who is wondrous in His righteous martyrs, among whom is Fr. Mina Abood Sharobeem.

To God be the glory forever. Amen.[25]

Mrs. Sarah Refaat explains the following astonishing miracle:

My husband works in the Beshay Steel Company in Alexandria. Within the same year of Fr. Mina's martyrdom, the company assigned him to transport a shipment of steel to the church of St. George in Al Arish, which was the same area in which Fr. Mina served. Emil, my husband, was traveling on the road, which was incredibly dangerous; terrorists inhabited

---

25 This account by Mrs. Mona Girgis Ramzy, as well as the following miracle by Mrs. Sarah Refaat, were transcribed from a video interview that took place at the home of Sister Mariam, recorded by an organization referred to as *Elahna Al Qawy* [Our Strong God], and shared here with their permission.

the desert through which the road ran, and they were known to stop Christians and kill them. Because of the dangers on the road, there were dozens of military checkpoints along the way; the officers would check the licenses of the travelers, interrogate them, and search their vehicles.

Emil was somewhat fearful; but I encouraged him, "Don't be afraid! Don't you know whose path you're travelling on? This is Fr. Mina's path! You're also going to visit St. George!" Every fifteen minutes I would call him and encourage him.

Suddenly, I found him calling me, explaining frantically that at one of the checkpoints, an officer switched his work permit with the permit of a non-Christian man. The latter had already driven off and taken my husband's work permit. Without proper identification, he would be unable to continue his drive to Al Arish, because there were many more military checkpoints left to pass through.

Emil was given a paper written by the officer who accidentally switched the permits. He instructed him, "Show this at every checkpoint so they can let you pass." Of course, my husband was doubtful that the paper would do its job, since the country was so unstable.

After ending the call, I stood at my window, looked up to the sky and began to talk to, or rather, boldly demand Fr. Mina to heed my requests. "Fr. Mina," I ordered, "you will bring my husband's permit back to him. You will protect him all throughout the way. You will not let a single officer stop him at any checkpoint."

After each checkpoint, he would call me and say, "They stopped every car behind me and in front of me. When it was my turn, they would immediately let me go, saying, 'Go in peace, may God guard your path.'" Each officer at each checkpoint said the same exact phrase. My husband drove a huge truck, carrying large amounts of steel, and yet they did not take a single look at his cargo!

He arrived at the church of St. George safely, and I advised him to let one of the priests there pray for him. It was nearing midnight, and Emil had planned to sleep in the church and begin the drive back to Alexandria in the morning. (After midnight, the military would close the roads).

He called me once more after midnight, saying, "I'll be sleeping in the desert tonight, since the church won't allow me to spend the night"—(he also had several non-Christians with him).

I responded, "Emil, you will leave for Alexandria now, and Fr. Mina will be with you."

He attempted to explain the situation—the roads were closed! And yet I was adamant and full of faith. I convinced him to begin the journey and urged him to invoke the prayers of Fr. Mina along that road; it was the very road along which he was martyred. By the grace of God, again, not a single officer stopped him, though his truck was the only vehicle on the entire desert road.

I did not sleep that night; I spent it in prayer, and in talking to Fr. Mina, confident that he would fulfill my requests. Six hours later, I received another call from him, and he was very fearful; his manager, an extremely difficult man, had gotten news that the work permit had been lost, and warned him that the missing permit meant he would possibly be fired and pay a three-thousand pound fine.

After hanging up with Emil, I petitioned Fr. Mina again, "You will get my husband's permit back, and he won't pay a penny!"

Upon arriving to Alexandria, and reaching the company, my husband was immediately called to the office of the manager, who was a non-Christian. Of course, Emil walked in feeling exceptionally anxious; his manager was notorious for firing any employee over the smallest error.

The manager proceeded to recount, "Earlier today a stranger came asking for me by name, and the doorkeeper guided him to my office. I brought him in and asked him what he wanted. He explained, 'When Emil comes, tell him I brought him his permit.' He pulled out your lost work permit from his pocket. I was both surprised and confused, and asked him, 'Who do I tell him came and brought it?' The man replied, 'He knows who I am.'"

My husband, thinking it somehow could have been the driver who took his permit back in Al Arish, asked, "Sir, would you mind describing to me what he looks like?"

To his shock, Emil was told, "The man was one of your priests. He was thin and young, maybe in his late thirties. He had a short black beard and mustache, and was tan-skinned. He wore a pair of brown glasses and had a comforting smile."

My husband's non-Christian manager had described, in full detail, Fr. Mina himself!

Sister Mariam shared the following miracle, sent to her by a European woman who remains anonymous:

> I lost my daughter three years ago while pregnant and had to deliver her stillborn and then bury her. Since then, the pain of her loss has been so great. Also, since that time, my husband and I have been trying to have another child. I would get pregnant and then miscarry very early. This happened three times over two years.
>
> Then we tried IVF, where the doctor told me it would be very difficult to get pregnant because my eggs are very few, and their quality is bad. We tried it anyway, I got pregnant and then miscarried again. Due to the hormones I was on, I developed clots in my lungs and was in the intensive care unit for a few days. The doctors told me I would have to be on blood thinners for a long time. I gave up all hope of having another baby and said that this was God's will. Six months later I learned that I was pregnant again. In my mind, I knew what would happen, but in my heart, I felt that this may be my miracle. The pregnancy was going well, then 2 months later I started to bleed and developed an infection.
>
> I cried to God and asked Him, "Why? Why

another heartache?"

I fell asleep and saw a priest standing at the back of a church waiting to greet me. He was dressed in his liturgical tunic and had a smile on his face. I approached him and told him in Arabic "Abouna [i.e. Father] pray for me. I'm ..."

He did not let me finish my sentence, and replied in Arabic with a beautiful comforting smile, "You're pregnant. Yes, I know. Do not be afraid."

I quickly woke up and told my husband what I saw.

He asked me who the priest was, I told him, "I don't know, I've never seen him before."

A few days later, I was on Facebook and suddenly saw the picture of this priest. Someone from my church had posted it. Tears quickly came to my eyes and I ran to my husband and told him, "This is him! This is the priest I saw in my dreams!"

I don't know how to read Arabic very well, so I asked my husband to read who he was and about him. It was the saint and martyr Fr. Mina Abood! That week the bleeding stopped, and the infection cleared with antibiotics. The doctors said everything looked perfect.

He became my intercessor for the entire pregnancy. If there was any doubt, any pain, any medication for the clots and for the diabetes I had to take, and when I fell at the end of the pregnancy, I asked for his help. And then finally, a few weeks ago, God granted me mercy and I gave birth to our miracle baby Cyril (Kyrillos) Mina. I thank God for introducing me to this great saint, whom I didn't know. May Fr. Mina protect us always and watch over us.

A young woman, who requested anonymity, explains an incredible miracle performed through Hieromartyr Mina's prayers:

In January of 2019, during a lab session, an optometry student found out from one of her professors that a lump was found inside her right eye. She was informed that it could potentially cause damage to certain parts of her eye. They sent her in to the clinic for additional testing to see if they could identify what it was.

After days of testing, it was agreed that they would monitor the growth before deciding on a course of treatment. Following a three-month recheck, they noticed very little growth. It would be ideal to hold off on any treatment and reevaluate everything in another three months.

In September of 2019, she went in for testing and realized the doctors were uneasy with the results; upon examination of all scans and photos, it was discovered that the lump had grown significantly and was now causing some problems to structures in the eye. The physicians suggested that she be seen by a specialist to verify the course of treatment, and possibly remove the lump. Terrified about what was to come next, she decided with her doctor to wait one more week, then undergo one last ultrasound before going to the specialist.

As the week progressed, a group of her colleagues and

friends decided to gather and pray the Midnight Praises in one of their apartments. To the surprise of all, one of those in attendance brought a reliquary containing the precious blood of Hieromartyr Mina Abood. All felt an unexplainable sense of peace and holiness permeating through the apartment, and the hymns were chanted angelically. It was felt as though this martyr stood among the faithful and praised with them.

After the praises were completed, this young woman headed over to the relics to receive a blessing. She was unaware of who the martyr in their midst was. She asked to privately venerate the relics in one of the apartment's rooms; she was granted her request. As she placed the reliquary on her eye, she did not utter a word, but instead wept and implored for the martyr's blessing.

Later that evening, all the youth gathered in a circle and were told about the blessed life that Fr. Mina led. The young woman could not believe the blessing that was right beside her. She asked her friend, the custodian of the relics, to entreat Fr. Mina on her behalf. He gave her a photo of the martyr with blessed spices to have with her at all times.

From that night onwards, she wrapped the picture on her eye, praying wholeheartedly that he may intercede for her and touch her eye with his healing hand.

Upon returning to lab the following week, a peer of hers was practicing a test on her right eye. Overlooking the peer was the same professor who first noticed the lump. Suddenly, her classmate stated that the findings were clear, and that all structures in the eye looked healthy. Confused about what she heard, she turned to the professor.

"It's impossible," she thought to herself, knowing that

just days prior, the lump was so large that none of the structures in the eye could even be identified.

The professor smiled and tapped her on the shoulder, telling her, "I saw, and I am telling you that everything looks all clear."

She instantly started crying, explaining the story to her friends who knew what she was going through. They all wept with her, shocked at the miracle that they had just witnessed.

That week, this woman met with her doctor, who looked at everything and spoke to the professor. All were speechless that the lump suddenly became non-existent without any medical intervention.

To this day, every time they perform the test on her, she takes a sigh of relief and smiles when she hears, "all clear."

May the blessings of Fr. Mina be with us all.

Statements In Commemoration of Hieromartyr Mina Abood

HIS HOLINESS POPE TAWADROS II

POPE OF ALEXANDRIA AND PATRIARCH OF THE SEE OF ST. MARK

"[The] Mother of the martyrs is beautiful, [the] Mother of the honorable is noble..." Such is the method by which the spiritual songs of our Coptic Orthodox Church address the righteous martyrs. The living Church gladly offers her children up to martyrdom, for the blood of the martyrs is the soundest evidence of the vivacity of the Church, and its permanence and germination.

The Church offers martyrs in every age, and in every region. In 1981, she offered up one of her honorable bishops, His Grace Bishop Samuel the general bishop, and through the years, she has offered men, women, youth, and children. In the events which our beloved Egypt undergoes in this month of July 2013, she has offered up Abanoub, a youth from Assiut. She has offered up Nardine, a young woman from Alexandria. Lastly, she has offered up Reverend Fr. Mina, a priest in Al Arish. All of them have gained the glorious crown of martyrdom as a result of their unfailing Christian faith, and in defense of the freedom of their country.

Fr. Mina Abood, who lived less than forty years on the earth, filled all of his years with love, instruction, service, deaconship, and priesthood. He lived as a student, a servant, a deacon, a priest, and as an incredible husband and father to an exceptional Christ-loving family.

Though his years were little, he was careful to fill them with love and ministry, and with toil and sacrifice before and after his priesthood. He served in the capacity of the holy priesthood for only a year and a few months, during which he strived in ministering to the students in the Diocese of North Sinai. He visited them at their universities, as well as in the church of St. Philopateer Mercurius in Al Arish. Many bishops, priests, deacons, servants, and congregants bear good witness of him.

As we bid him farewell on the hope of the resurrection,

we also bid farewell to the good example he set, the very example which made His Grace Bishop Cosman, bishop of the Diocese of North Sinai, choose him for the priesthood in his diocese. He discovered in him the qualities of the kindness of heart and of the aroma of Christ. He appointed him to his own secretariat in the diocese, in addition to the pastoral responsibilities he was to carry out among the youth. This portrays His Grace's unequivocal confidence in the priest he ordained.

We entreat Christ our God to accept back the great gift He once let live among us, the very gift which has now been crowned with the crown of martyrdom. We entreat that He may grant comfort to his virtuous wife, Sister Mariam, to his blessed daughters, as well as to his blessed bishop, His Grace Bishop Cosman, his brothers the priests, to all his loved ones and children, and to all who have become familiarized with his goodness and love.

May the grace of Christ encompass us all.

HIS EMINENCE METROPOLITAN HEDRA

METROPOLITAN OF THE DIOCESE OF ASWAN
AND ABBOT OF THE GREAT MONASTERY
OF ST. PACHOMIUS OF THE KOINONIA

To a loving and beloved father,

The Church in its entirety now bids you farewell, O

blessed, loving, and beloved Reverend Fr. Mina Abood Sharobeem. You were born in the city of Aswan to a truly pious Christian family, one bound to the Church and to her fathers in a bond of love, intimacy, and profound pursuit after the spiritual matters. Here you were raised, and here you grew little by little. You matured within this family, which was wholly attached to the church of St. Mary in Aswan. In this church, you became an exemplary deacon, serving the altar of God in vigor and reverence to the Holy Gifts which sit upon it. You served in purity, maintaining a spirit of holiness and a manner of life which all can attest follows the commandments of our Lord, God, and Savior Jesus Christ [as] written in the holy gospels.

You adored the Church, holding her in the highest esteem, loving her and all that is in her—specifically, her beautiful, comforting hymns. You excelled in learning them, chanting them in your God-given angelic voice. Thus, in your mastery of hymnology, and your continual attendance of the Midnight Praises on the eve of Sunday in the church of St. Mary, you surpassed many, and you remained with us until your matriculation into the University of Ain Shams. So, as a dove, you flew to where you can spread your wings and expand your service. There, in Cairo, you founded the [Hymns] School of St. Stephen the Archdeacon and Protomartyr. Your growing adoration of the altar rendered you worthy to become chosen to the holy priesthood, and from there your desires to pursue that which is holy made you worthy of martyrdom.

Truly I have witnessed you become as the Thrice-blessed Bishop Makary of Sinai, whose manner of departure from the world was in the manner of martyrdom. I have witnessed you become as he whom you loved, St. Stephen.

You have gained both the crown of priesthood and that of martyrdom. For this, the entire Church bids you farewell with a spirit of comfort, a spirit of strength, and a spirit of victory. Those closest to you display all of this, especially your dear and holy wife. She comprehended your heart's longing to become united to the person of our Lord Jesus Christ. You wished to take on His example, as said by our teacher Paul the Apostle: "looking unto Jesus, the author and finisher of our faith, who for the joy that was set before Him endured the cross, despising the shame, and has sat down at the right hand of the throne of God" (Heb 12:2).

Therefore, blessed are you; you have arrived speedily into the bosom of our fathers the saintly martyrs, up in the highest heavenly ranks. We ask you to remember us, your church and congregation, and all those who love you, your sacred life, and your very blessed departure from this vain world.

Remember my weaknesses, that the Lord may help me as He has helped you.

HIS GRACE BISHOP MOUSSA

GENERAL BISHOP

Intercede for us, O our father the martyr!

I beg Fr. Mina, as he stands before the throne of grace, to remember that, at one point, he served with us here in this fleeting world. Though his years were few in number, they were immensely fruitful. He served in St. Mary's church in Al Amiriya, and later his services spanned, through his work in St. Mark's Festival, to reach the entire Coptic world, inside and outside Egypt. Now, his services span the whole Church, in Egypt and the diaspora, in Paradise and on earth, offering prayers and intercessions on our behalf at all times. Our valuable father, you remain in our hearts. Your name was Saleeb, after that very cross of ministry which you faithfully carried. Blessed are you. I ask you to pray for me.

HIS GRACE BISHOP RAPHAEL

GENERAL BISHOP

Reverend Fr. Mina Abood Sharobeem, the servant and priest of Al Arish, has gained the crown of martyrdom after being fired upon before his church. I personally knew Fr. Mina during his service with us, and I remember his angelic demeanor. May the Lord accept Fr. Mina's prayers on our behalf, as He accepted the sacrifice he offered for the sake of His holy name. Lucky you!

HIS GRACE BISHOP MACARIUS

BISHOP OF AL MINYA

"Our friend Lazarus sleeps…"

I became acquainted with Fr. Mina five years ago when I began my supervision of the church of St. Mary. He was tranquil in nature, a man of few words, and a lover of hymnology and praises. He was able to disciple many from those in the surrounding region. When the church decided on those who would receive the grace of the holy priesthood, he was among those who were nominated for ordination; although our plan was to offer him up for ordination in the future, the Lord God decided on an alternative place, one with a better and more diverse ministry awaiting him. Therefore, He called him to serve in the Diocese of North Sinai with His Grace Bishop Cosman, who appointed him as a secretary in addition to his priestly duties. And the Lord willed to number him with those in the ranks of the martyrs, and from there, he became a blessing to the Church as a whole.

What distinguishes the Coptic Orthodox Church is that she is a Church of martyrs. She has offered, and continues to offer on a daily basis, millions of martyrs, confessors, and saints. Presently, every Christian in Egypt carries a death sentence, preparing to witness to Christ at any moment. Moreover, the Copts take pride in their fathers the martyrs, desiring to obtain this blessing and honor in similitude of those who went before them.

We ask for comfort to his virtuous wife and young daughters, and to His Grace Bishop Cosman, bishop of

North Sinai. We ask for comfort to the assembly of priests in Al Arish, to the entire church of St. Mary in Al Amiriya, where he began to grow in his ministry, to every family member, spiritual child, and to all his loved ones.

Though Fr. Mina has become hidden from our physical eyes, he is incessantly present in our hearts and consciences. He has become an intercessor and ambassador on our behalf, asking for us till we complete our struggle in peace.

HEGUMEN RAPHAEL ABBA MINA

"And God will wipe away every tear from their eyes" (Rev 7:17; 21:4)

The Lord God has crowned our beloved Fr. Mina Abood, who now rests in the bosom of our Lord Jesus Christ, with the crown of eternal life. He who granted him a heart of purity and uprightness now wipes away every tear from his eyes. The Holy Lord whom he served in virtue and sincerity now bestows upon him the crowns of priesthood, righteousness, and martyrdom.

In him we saw seriousness in the spiritual life, faithfulness in the ministry, and meekness and lowliness. He adored the fathers here in the Monastery of St. Mina, and so, he gained the love of all.

Now he has been called to serve in a much greater capacity—within the bosom of the Lord. There, he entreats [the Lord] for his blessed family, that He may comfort them with His Holy Spirit, allowing them to become shining lampstands, leading good lives, for the glory of His name. He entreats [God] for his Church, his congregants, and for all Christians across Egypt and the diaspora, that the Lord may protect them with His holy and pure angels, inscribing their names in the Book of Eternal Life. Amen.

HEGUMEN DAOUD LAMEI

Our saintly father: Blessed are you! Blessed are you!

You have preceded us to Paradise. You have entered crowned with crowns of service, pastoral care, and most elegant of them all, the crown of martyrdom. The very treacherous bullets used against you have become a means for you to share in the passions of Christ; they have become the print of His nails in your pure body. You have become as your namesake and intercessor, St. Mina the Wonderworker, who was martyred in his youth and became a lampstand for the entire world.

You left an example for all those who knew you, those who served with you, and those who enjoyed your friendship; the very minutes of our lives carry gravity and meaning. Oh, how transitory this life has become! Thousands of priests currently look to you in marvel; you have gained the crown of martyrdom before them and your heart was selected before the hearts of many.

Pray for us, O man of God. Pray for us, O beloved of

Christ, O martyr of the twenty-first century. Intercede for us, O the pride of the Church, O the chosen flower of the holy priesthood. Remember us before the Lord, that He may forgive us our sins.

SISTER MARIAM

To My Husband the Martyr

To the soul of my father, my love, my husband, Fr. Mina:

I was able to grasp how sweet of an individual you were, both inside and out. Life was as enjoyable as can possibly be with you by my side. Your companionship was the most pleasant thing. Your heart overflowed with tenderness, making you capable of harboring the most beautiful qualities, which attracted me to you more and more every single day. I learned so much from you.

But never could I have imagined seeing you as a valiant martyr, a mighty saint, and a powerful intercessor, pleading on behalf of many. O you who wished to remain hidden from the eyes of men, preferring to silently minister to your flock without being noticed, have now become an advocate to countless loved ones and spiritual children.

I want to congratulate you on meriting the true joy that is found only in the depths of Paradise. I want to congratulate you on the eternal rest you now find yourself in, surrounded by "the angels and saints in the glories of heaven," as you have come and related to me time and time again.

May you forever continue to minister to us. May we forever continue to sense your compassionate fatherhood and your pleadings before the divine throne.

Remember all of your children, those who implore your prayers and seek you with hope.

Remember your daughters, Verina and Youstina, and remember us all.

Until we meet again, you will continually be the crown on my head, my glory, and the greatest gift given to me by the hand of our Lord Jesus Christ, to whom be the glory and honor, both now and forever. Amen.

Your wife,

Mariam

Thank you to those who have tirelessly labored with love in producing this groundbreaking biography. I wish that our Lord Jesus may reward their labors of love with joys and many blessings, both here on earth, and in heaven.

"Those who are wise shall shine like the brightness of the firmament, and those who turn many to righteousness like the stars forever and ever" (Dan 12:3)

Bibliography

Irvine, C. (2013, July 6). *Egypt: Coptic Christian Priest Shot Dead.* The Telegraph. https://www.telegraph.co.uk/news/worldnews/africaandindianocean/egypt/10164062/Egypt-Coptic-Christian-priest-shot-dead.html

Johnson, A. (2013, July 15). *Muslim Extremists Kill Our Priests, Burn Our Churches and Kidnap Our Women: How Egypt's Arab Spring Dream Descended into a Nightmare of Religious Hatred.* Pravmir. https://www.pravmir.com/muslim-extremists-kill-our-priests-burn-our-churches-and-kidnap-our-women-how-egypts-arab-spring-dream-descended-into-a-nightmare-of-religious-hatred/

Masraa Rajul Din Masihiyu Be Rusas Musalahin Fi Al-Arish [Killing of a Christian Cleric by Gunmen in Al-Arish]. (2013, July 6). MBC [video broadcast station offered by satellite and other live streaming mediums]. Original news broadcast of Fr. Mina's murder; supplied by Mina Nathan. Used with permission.

Middleton, P. (2011). *Martyrdom: A Guide for the Perplexed.* T&T Clark International.

Milad, M. (2018). *Arish Martyrs.* ME Sat [video broadcast station offered by satellite and other live streaming mediums]. Cairo, Egypt, 2018. Used with permission.

Milad, M. (2019). *Shafi' Jideed* [A New Intercessor Saint]. Live Print Publishing House..

Muslim Brotherhood. (2019 May 2020). Encyclopedia Britannica.. www.britannica.com/topic/Muslim-Brotherhood

Nathan, M. (Director) (2014). *Al-Kahin Al-Shahid* [The Priest Martyr] [Documentary Film] [also available at: https://www.youtube.com/watch?v=wP4Zy3SyXPs]. Used with permission.

Nicene and Post-Nicene Fathers: First Series, Philip Schaff, ed. (1886–1889; reprinted frequently).

St. Theophan the Recluse (1994). *Kindling the Divine Spark.* Saint Herman Press.

CPSIA information can be obtained
at www.ICGtesting.com
Printed in the USA
JSHW041455270323
39470JS00004B/211